Sue –
I hope you enjoy
this book! We're so
glad you went with
us to the Holy Land.
you may recognize
some of chapter 10:
We're keeping you in
Prayer –
God bless you,
Randy
Childress

A.I.M. for High Ground
The Adventure in Ministry

True Stories of Leadership in Crisis and in Joy

*Since, then, you have been raised with Christ, set your hearts on
things above, where Christ is, seated at the right hand of God.
Set your minds on things above, not on earthly things.*

Colossians 3:1–2

Randall R. Childress

WESTBOW
PRESS®
A DIVISION OF THOMAS NELSON
& ZONDERVAN

I have tried to recreate events, locales and conversations from my memories of them. In order to maintain their anonymity in some instances I have changed the names of individuals and places, I may have changed some identifying characteristics and details such as physical properties, occupations and places of residence.

WestBow Press books may be ordered through booksellers or by contacting:

WestBow Press
A Division of Thomas Nelson & Zondervan
1663 Liberty Drive
Bloomington, IN 47403
www.westbowpress.com
1 (866) 928-1240

All Scripture quotations, unless otherwise indicated, are taken from the Holy Bible, New International Version®, NIV®. Copyright ©1973, 1978, 1984, 2011 by Biblica, Inc.™ Used by permission of Zondervan. All rights reserved worldwide. www.zondervan.com The "NIV" and "New International Version" are trademarks registered in the United States Patent and Trademark Office by Biblica, Inc.™

Scripture quotations marked (NKJV) are taken from the New King James Version®. Copyright © 1982 by Thomas Nelson. Used by permission. All rights reserved.

ISBN: 978-1-9736-6701-8 (sc)
ISBN: 978-1-9736-6702-5 (hc)
ISBN: 978-1-9736-6700-1 (e)

Library of Congress Control Number: 2019908421

Print information available on the last page.

WestBow Press rev. date: 7/2/2019

Contents

Acknowledgments

A special thanks to my editor, Brittany Clarke, whose efficiency, professionalism and encouragement kept me working on this project. Brittany was easy to work with. If God blesses this book and allows me to write another, I will knock on Brittany's email door for editing. Thanks Brittany.

Thanks to all the elders I have worked with over the years. I'm grateful for their patience.

I'm especially grateful to the elders I served with at Kempsville Christian Church in over thirty years of wonderful ministry. Some have already gone to the Lord, but I'm grateful to them all. Their support and encouragement is something *every* minister should have.

My love and gratitude to my wife, Sandra, and our three sons who supported both my ministry and the work of the church.

Most of all, my gratitude to the Lord for a wonderful life, family and church.

Introduction

You've seen those disclaimers at the beginning of a movie or TV show: "The following is based on actual events. Only the names, locations, and events have been changed." You instinctively know some of what you see is true and some has been added as filler for context.

This book is a memoir of my experiences in ministry. While I may not be able to recall all the words in every conversation, most of these events and conversations did take place. Many of the names and locations have been changed to respect the privacy of individuals. Some circumstances were adapted and filler was added to chapter 2 for development.

I have called this book *A.I.M. for High Ground: The Adventure in Ministry.* I would like everyone to know how exciting the ministry really is. Far from living in an "ivory tower," protected from problems and challenges, ministers are confronted with nearly every facet of life. For six years I helped my father operate three shoe stores in three cities. I know the challenges that come along with the secular marketplace. However, nothing has challenged me as much as Christian ministry has.

One of the greatest challenges is working with people who voluntarily connect themselves with your ministry.

One of the greatest *blessings* is working with people who voluntarily connect themselves with your ministry.

The most fulfilling and gratifying blessing is serving God.

The most exciting blessing is watching people come to Christ.

I hope the stories in this book will convey the challenges, victories, and disappointments that come when working with God's people.

1. The first chapter, "The Gates of Hell Shall Not Prevail," demonstrates how opportunities to serve God often come at the most inopportune times.

2. "The Greatest Resource in a Church" shows that our greatest physical resource in ministry is not money, equipment, or facilities.

3. "How Long Must I Put Up With Them?" is a question many in Christian leadership ask. We might be surprised who else felt that way.

4. "Demonism?" helps us make good judgment about people and appreciate older, more experienced Christians.

5. "Beware the Media" tells of my own experience and gives several tips to understand and utilize media.

6. In "Facing Death in the Congregation," I describe various kinds of death from my experience. One in particular strengthened my faith.

7. "Virtue: Personal Responsibility" was the most difficult chapter for me to write, as it gives examples of disappointing moral failures within churches I served.

8. "The Two Most Influential Men in My Life" is what it sounds like; it tells about the two men who influenced me the most in my life.

9. In "The Best Definitions of Leadership," I describe what I have learned about dedicated Christian leaders from the churches I have served.

10. Finally, in "Every Christian Should Go to the Holy Land; Every Preacher MUST Go to the Holy Land," I give reasons to motivate every Christian to make this trip.

It is also my hope that church leaders will benefit from my experiences and that perhaps young people reading this book will be encouraged to enter ministry and enjoy the same profession I have for forty-five years.

At the end of most chapters, I have included a brief summary of lessons I learned and a series of questions I hope will aid in the reader's reflection.

My wife asked me what the purpose of this book would be. "To leave something behind," I said. Ultimately, it is my desire to leave a legacy from nearly five decades of ministry that honors the Lord. Please be patient with me, for I am still on the journey.

Bio: Randall Childress

Over forty-five years of ministry, I have served churches in both Virginia, and Tennessee. My wife Sandi and I have been married forty-seven years and have three sons: Todd, Josh, and Jonathan. Josh is a minister, while Todd and Jonathan serve in volunteer ministries. Sandi and I enjoy 6 delightful grandchildren.

Dedication

I want to dedicate this book to the most influential men in my life:

Ralph Childress

Clarence Greenleaf

The Gates of Hell Will Not Prevail

Eight hours doesn't seem like much, just one third of a day, less than the average workday for many people, but for Melanie, it was over 500 miles from home. With the loneliness she felt now, it might as well have been a million miles.

Deep in her heart, Melanie knew it didn't have to be this way. It shouldn't be this way. She was a twenty-two-year-old woman with a six-week-old baby. They were alone, just she and her child, destitute. Her father had warned her, but it was too late to change things now.

Living in a small town in Ohio, Melanie was a quiet, unpretentious child who mostly kept to herself. She wasn't as outgoing as other girls her age, and boys didn't ask her for dates. By the time she reached twenty, she felt left out, that life was "passing her by." Other girls her age were engaged, and some were already married. Still living at home with her parents, she felt her life was wasting away . . . that she was missing out.

Without her parent's knowledge, she had started going to a singles club on weekends hoping to make friends and maybe meet a boy who, like her, was looking for a relationship. It didn't take long.

After two weeks her father learned where she was going and confronted her. "This is NO place for someone like you to go!" he insisted. She maintained that she just wanted to make friends. "No," he said, "when you go to a garbage dump all you find is trash and rats! Stay away from there!" This led to a shouting match until . . .

"I'M OLD ENOUGH TO MAKE MY OWN DECISIONS!" Melanie shouted.

"YOU'RE OLD ENOUGH TO BE OUT ON YOUR OWN TOO!" her father countered.

Melanie spun on her heels and stormed out the door, slamming it behind her. She didn't know where she was going, but she was determined to be her own person. She was twenty-two and needed to be independent.

She pulled out her cell phone, one her father had provided for her safety, to call Jimmy, a boy she had met at the singles club, to ask or advice. She would now use the phone to spite her father.

Jimmy welcomed Melanie into his one-bedroom apartment, saying he would sleep on the couch. A few months later, Melanie realized she was pregnant. She wanted to be excited . . . she wanted to call her parents and tell them the news, but she dared not. She hadn't spoken to them since she stormed out. So, she decided to leave them out of it, but she couldn't wait to share the news with Jimmy.

Jimmy, on the other hand, was not happy with the news. He had plans of his own. A new job had opened up in Virginia, and it was a great opportunity for him. He didn't want to miss it.

"We'll go with you. You don't have to miss that job. I'll help you with the move, and I'll make sure the baby isn't a problem."

Jimmy straightened up tall in a defiant stance and glared at her. His patience waning, he looked at her as if she was an inconvenience and said grudgingly, "Okay, we'll try it for a while."

Now, suddenly, Melanie felt a distance widening between them. Nonetheless, she went with him to Virginia, leaving her family and hometown behind.

Ten months later, the baby had come and Jimmy had had enough. Starting a new job was difficult and demanding without having to navigate around Melanie and the baby in their small apartment. It was getting on his nerves. He became angry when the baby cried at night. He thought Melanie showed too much attention to the newborn and he talked as if their baby were an intruder in their home. One thing led to another, until a shouting match caused the neighbor in the apartment next door to start banging on the wall.

"HEY! Hold it down in there! I'll call the super!"

Finally, Jimmy told her to get out. He didn't want either of them. He hadn't asked her to come, and now she had to go.

"But where will we go? What will we do?"

"That's your problem! You're on your own!"

*****

Now, with a backpack, a baby bag on one shoulder, a small duffel bag on the other, and little Stevie cradled in her left arm, Melanie was pacing the aisles of a local drug store pretending to be a shopper. It was late August and Virginia Beach was terribly humid. Perspiration rolled down both her and her baby's cheeks. She only had three bottles of formula, and the baby was already feeding on one.

With her arms loaded, she couldn't wipe away her tears. When people approached, she would look away, but most people would have mistaken the tears for drops of sweat.

Lynda, however, couldn't help but notice a young girl loaded down, carrying a baby and crying. "Are you all right, sweetie?"

"Yes. I'm fine. Thank you."

"That's a handsome young man in your arms," Lynda offered.

"Thank you. He's six weeks old." Her eyes welled up again.

Lynda placed her hand gently on Melanie's shoulder. "Are you sure you're all right? Things don't look like they're all right . . . Are you homeless?"

"I am *now*. My boyfriend and I moved here from Ohio. We had a big fight, and he kicked me out. I don't know what I'm going to do."

Lynda reached into her purse, pulled out a twenty-dollar bill, and stuffed it in Melanie's bag. "This is all the cash I have on me right now. But listen, about a mile away is the church I attend, Kempsville Christian. Go there, they'll help. Right now I have to pick up my mother for her doctor's appointment. I'm sorry I can't do more, but when I get Mom home, I'll come back here. If you're still here, we'll figure things out. Okay?"

Melanie nodded. At the word *mother*, she began to tear up again wishing her mother were with her now.

As Lynda walked out of the store, Melanie reshuffled the bags on her shoulders and picked up a pack of baby formula. She was starting toward the cashier, when a large woman approached her.

"Listen, I couldn't help but hear what you guys said. I know you're in trouble, and I want to help. My name is Sam. That's short for Samantha. 'Samantha' is too feminine for a woman with *my* disposition, so I go by Sam. What's your name, honey?"

Melanie timidly lowered her eyes. "Melanie." Nodding toward her baby, she said, "This is Stevie."

"Melanie, I have a place big enough to take you and Stevie in. He'll have plenty of room to crawl around when he gets bigger. And I've got plenty of food." She smiled and patted her stomach with both hands, "You can see I like to eat. You're welcome to come home with me."

Melanie was startled by this offer from a stranger. Sam could see she was struggling with the decision and decided to lay it all out for her.

"Look, here's the deal. You won't even have to pay rent for the first year, not until you find a job and a place of your own, but you need to know something. I'm a Satanist. I've been sent here from New York to start a satanic chapter in Virginia Beach. Every now and then a couple of members may come by, but I promise you and your child will be safe.

Melanie became frightened and frustrated at the same time. Her mind couldn't process this quickly enough. It started clouding up, and she was afraid she might faint.

Finally, she answered. "Thank you. Your offer is very kind. But first . . . would you mind driving me by Kempsville Christian? Lynda may have called them . . . they may be waiting on me."

Sam smiled and said, "Sure! I heard her say it's a mile down the road. C'mon, let's go."

*****

Most preachers feel the pressure of the Sunday sermon on Saturday evening, not Sunday morning. We may have worked on the sermon all week long, but we want Saturday to pray, read, practice, and meditate on the next morning's message. Saturday evening is the time to work out the kinks, memorize the main points, and polish the delivery. That pressure is one of the reasons why I tried to protect Saturday evening from interference.

However, on this Saturday, Sandi and I had taken our sons to the beach for the day. It was a very hot and humid August day in Virginia Beach. The car's digital thermometer read 99 degrees outside, but the humidity must have kicked the heat index up to at least 103.

Sitting out in the sun and baking all day is not really my idea of relaxation. I'm fair skinned. I burn and peel, then burn and peel again. Of Hawaiian descent, my wife, on the other hand, tans beautifully. Not only that, but the sun and heat have a way of sapping energy out of me, so I was looking forward to getting back to an air-conditioned home and preparing for Sunday morning. However, God had other plans.

When we turned onto our street, a van covered with satanic graffiti was ominously parked in front of the house.. My shock quickly turned to anger. "Why on earth would anyone park *that* in front of the parsonage?" Our sons in the back seat sat up wide-eyed to see what I was upset about.

"That's terrible. Who would drive something like that?" Sandi muttered.

The black van with red and yellow artwork featured swastikas, pitchforks, and horned goats. A large inverted red pentagram was flaunted on both sides, confirming both the van and the driver were advertising bad news.

Along with my anger was a tinge of embarrassment. The parsonage is located on a quiet street behind the church building and next to a public elementary school. The school grounds were always busy, even on weekends. Everyone using the school's basketball courts or ball field would have seen the van parked in front of the parsonage. This vehicle did not convey the image I was trying to set for the community.

As we pulled into the driveway, I noticed there were two women sitting in the front seats of the van. A young woman on the passenger side exited the van holding a baby. I sent my wife and children into the house and walked toward the road to meet her.

"Are you the minister of this church?" she asked.

"Yes, I'm Randy Childress." I looked back at the woman still in the van. "What can I do for you?"

"I hope you can help me," she said. "I don't know what to do. I've been evicted, and I don't have anywhere to go. I don't have any money, and I only have a little formula for the baby. Can you help?"

"How did you happen to come here?" Our church building is located in a community off the main road. Normally, vagrants would travel up and down a busy highway visiting those church buildings, but she would have had to intentionally come to Kempsville.

"I was afraid. I didn't know what to do," she pointed to her right, "so I just was walking through the drug store at the intersection to stay in air conditioning. Then I just broke down and started crying. That's when Sam approached me." She nodded to the other woman in the van.

The woman sitting on the driver's side was a watching us very closely with a cheeky smirk on her face. I'm not sure, but I felt she was watching *me* in particular. She couldn't hear what Melanie and I were saying, but it was as if she knew nonetheless. Her stare was intimidating.

"Who *is* that?" I asked.

"That's Sam. Her real name is Samantha, but she goes by Sam. Sam offered to take me to her home, but I'm afraid to go with her. She's a Satanist, and she told me if I went to her place there would be others there and they would try to recruit me. I asked her to bring me here first."

"Here?" I didn't recognize her, but it was possible she could have attended one of our worship services here.

"Have you attended here before?"

"No, but I met another lady, before Sam, who *is* a member of the church. When I told her the trouble I was in and that I didn't know where to turn, she told me this church helped the homeless."

I sighed. Actually, it was more of a huff. I was exhausted from the day at the beach, sunburned, and frustrated with the interruption to my schedule. I wanted to rest, clean up, and start studying my sermon for the next morning.

"Look," I said, "we *do* help people on occasion, but we have a committee who does this. Come back tomorrow morning and I'll introduce you to them."

Her face and shoulders dropped at the same time.

At that moment, Sam opened the door and stepped out of the van. She had an imposing stature and the appearance of someone who had "been there and done that," someone who had done it all. She didn't need to wait for Melanie to tell her my answer; she could read it in Melanie's expression. And she couldn't wait to taunt me.

Close to six feet tall, she was a big woman. Stout, but not fat. *Probably has six brothers who're wrestlers*, I thought. She had a very short spiked haircut and was wearing dirty jeans and an oversized plaid shirt with the sleeves cut out. Tattoo sleeves with satanic images went up both arms and protruded from the collar of her shirt. . . and she was grinning.

"I told her you wouldn't do anything," she gloated.

"You what?" I wear hearing aids and sometimes don't hear correctly, but that wasn't the case here. I was just thickheaded.

"I said, I told her you wouldn't do anything!"

They say your whole life passes before you when you die. I don't know about that, but I now know what happens at the point of genuine conviction . . . your guilt clobbers you in the head. In that moment I forgot where we were, what we were talking about, and to whom I was talking. My mind careened out of my control. I couldn't think about the schoolyard or the neighbors or the church or anything . . . other than what just happened. It was like watching a TV program when the camera zooms in on a particular subject and everything else blurs out. Stunned, I was speechless for maybe the first time in my life.

While I was still processing it all, Sam leaned in and snapped her fingers in front of my eyes.

"Hello! Earth calling! Anyone home?"

I felt the blood rush to my face, not from anger, but from shame. Now, I was more ashamed of myself than at any other time in my life. I had considered this desperate young mother nothing more than an inconvenience in my routine. My life didn't pass before my eyes, but sermons, Scripture passages, and public statements I had made began to rush through my mind. Realization set in.

I was more like the religious hypocrites than like Jesus. More like the selfish, insensitive priest and Levite than the Good Samaritan.

How many sermons had I preached on compassion? How many times had I admonished the church that we must look beyond ourselves to see Jesus in the needs of others? Jesus, the one who said, "Whatever you did for the least of these, you did for me." How many times had I challenged the church to follow Jesus' example?

How often I reminded them that Jesus stopped to help the diseased woman in the midst of a mission, that He stopped in a busy crowd to help a paralytic and a blind person. How many times I'd said, "The only way we're going to change this world is to live out the life of Christ before it!"

And yet, now, I had essentially told this young, desperate mother, "Go away. I don't have time for you." I must have been busier than Jesus. The next few seconds felt like hours as all these thoughts rushed through my mind.

I remembered an experience my preacher, Clarence Greenleaf, told me of years earlier. One Saturday afternoon a woman knocked on his door and asked for money to buy food. He gave her a few dollars, bid her well, and closed the door. As he stormed back to his study, he said, "I can't feed the whole world!" His wife Louise responded, "The whole world didn't ask you to feed it, just one woman in need." Preacher G said he was conscience-stricken and he vowed before God never to put his schedule before the needs of people. I should have learned more from his mentorship.

Sam waved her hand in front of my eyes and brought me back to the present. "Hello? Are you in there?"

Snapping to my senses, I said, "I'm sorry. You're absolutely right." Now *Sam* was stunned and the smirk faded.

I turned to Melanie. "Melanie, I'm so sorry. You will stay with us tonight. Come with me." Then, turning to Sam, I said. "Sam, if you'll wait a minute, I'll be right back."

I took Melanie in the house, and my wife prepared a room and spread a blanket to let the baby lie down. While Stevie drifted off to sleep with a pacifier, Sandi and Melanie went in the kitchen to make sandwiches and get acquainted.

When I came back outside, Sam was standing right where I'd left her. She looked shell-shocked. I said, "Let's go over to the office where we can talk."

Less than a hundred yards from the parsonage was the church building, and my office was just inside the door. During the entire trek, Sam walked beside me, her head lowered, deep in thought, and she was silent. The cynicism and bravado had disappeared.

My office was a converted classroom measuring twelve by twelve feet. Bookshelves covered three of the four walls bearing books I had collected over the past twenty-or-so years. My ordination certificate was proudly displayed on the wall behind me, and on each wall hung pictures of my wife and children. Religious pictures were also scattered throughout the room. My desk was covered with papers and files. I sat behind it trying to somehow mitigate my previous words and actions. If I ever intended to be a good influence on Sam, my work was cut out for me. I had lost ground earlier but now would do my best to make it up. In my heart I prayed, "Dear Lord, I'm sorry. I need you now."

Sam slumped into a chair in front of my desk. Her head was still lowered, and her eyes darted from side to side. It was as if she was weighing a multitude of different options in her mind. She was looking at a roadmap with a dot labelled *You are here* with hundreds of roads leading away in different directions. Which one would she choose? I sat quietly and waited for her to collect herself.

After a pause, she raised her head and spoke. "I . . . don't know what to do." Her emphasis was on *I*. Now *Sam* was afraid.

"What do you mean?"

"The others . . . back at the house . . . they **know** I had her. They're waiting for us."

"Who are 'they,' and why did they expect Melanie to come back with **you**?"

Then Sam told me her life's story. She and the others were members of a satanic cult in New York. They had been sent to Virginia Beach to establish a satanic cell here, and as they did, they were to recruit members. They had gone through an extensive training period to do this. The satanic cult would provide the resources to allow them full-time service. "And . . . there is accountability," she said. She looked at me, and I knew what she meant. Some kind of punishment would follow failure.

I knew very little about the Satan church. However, I did know most Satanists didn't particularly worship the devil; they simply used the image of the devil to represent their opposition to faith—any faith. In the Bible,

Satan is called "the adversary" (I Peter 5:8). That description suited their purpose.

I also knew as a devil's cult, they were dangerous. Richard Ramirez, the "Nightstalker," who murdered fourteen people in the mid-Eighties, claimed to be a Satanist. David Berkowitz, "the Son of Sam," also claimed to be a Satanist. I had read news reports of Satanists burning down church buildings and of decapitated animals found in various cities believed to have been used in animal sacrifices. While I didn't know much, I knew enough to tread carefully.

Sam continued, "When I saw Melanie standing in the aisle of the drug store crying, I knew she was in trouble and would be an easy mark for recruitment. She told me her boyfriend had kicked her and the baby out, that she was from Ohio and he had brought her here because he had a job lined up. She had no money, no family, and no friends. She had nowhere to go tonight, so, I told her she could come back and stay with me and my friends. We would take care of her and give her food to eat."

"So, the two of you had never met before? She had no way of knowing you were a Satanist?" I asked.

Sam became defensive. "Oh, I told her right up front that we were Satanists and she could expect to hear about our faith while she was with us."

"Then what?"

Sam took in a deep breath and let it out. "Then she asked me to bring her here. She said if she couldn't find help here, she would go with me. I agreed . . . I didn't think you would do anything. All the churches I've known only care about themselves . . . their own members."

That hit me hard. "Sam, to be honest, that's the way I was an hour ago. I wasn't very Christian out there with you and Melanie . . . I'm sorry. Melanie and the baby are going to stay with us tonight, and tomorrow we'll see how we can help her. You don't have to worry about them."

Now Sam looked worried. "But you don't understand. *They know* she was with me. If I don't bring her back, there will be *a terrible price to pay.*"

"What will they do to you?"

Her eyes were wide now, and her head was turning from one direction to the other as she spelled out the things satanic followers could do. "They could kick me out . . . deny my food rations . . . beat me up . . . they could even kill me!" Then, she looked straight at me. "We're not talkin' about saints here!"

"So, what can we do for *you*? How can we help *you*?"

Sam looked at me for the longest time. It seemed as though she were looking right through my eyes into my heart, trying to judge whether or not I was genuine.

"Tell me about this Jesus thing," she said.

That was *not* what I expected. After I realized she wasn't going to add anything to that request, I relaxed, smiled at her, picked up my Bible, came around the desk, and sat in the chair next to her.

She pushed my Bible away. "I already know what you're going to show me in that book. We had to memorize much of the Bible before they sent us out. We're trained to argue with it. I probably know the Bible better than most of your church members do." She nodded toward me. "Maybe even better than you!" Sure enough, she started quoting many scriptures I would have pointed her to, scriptures *with* the references.

"What I want to know," she said, "is why *YOU* believe it."

She wasn't going to accept a canned presentation of the gospel. So, we spent the next half hour in conversation about *MY* faith. I told her I had grown up in a Christian home with loving Christian parents. I had gone to college and majored in biology, which drew me to a study of creation science. More and more, by observation, experience, and facts, my faith was strengthened.

I told her after I left college, the preacher I grew up with asked me to help with the church youth program. I enjoyed working with people and teaching the Word of God. Eventually, I was led to full-time Christian ministry, and I had no regrets.

Even though I had relaxed somewhat, I thought at any moment she would challenge my faith and try to recruit *me!* That's what cultists do; they're trained to argue and refute any objection. *That* would have been a feather in her cap, wouldn't it? *Sam leads long-standing preacher to accept Satanism.* But, none of her questions or statements were challenges. She genuinely wanted to know why I would "forsake the pleasures of sin" she lived for to follow Jesus.

"And Jesus? Do you believe in Him because your parents did?"

I wondered about that, then answered, "Yes, I think at first I did. But as I grew older and learned more, I came to believe in Christ for my own reasons. I have no regret there either."

"What *were* those reasons? I already know about the resurrection. Don't bother with that. What else?"

"Well, even though I wasn't a drunkard or into the drug scene, I knew my heart was selfish. I hadn't committed so-called 'big sins' that people think about, but I was a sinner nonetheless. And I'm convinced that we're more than flesh and blood, that we have spirits that live on after death. Yet, I came to the realization that no matter how much good I might do in the future, I couldn't erase the sins I had committed in the past. Only Christ could do that. He is my only hope for heaven."

"That's where I am," she said, "hopeless. I *have* committed those big sins you're talkin' about. I'm so dirty, God doesn't want me. You wouldn't believe—"

"Sam, you don't have to tell me anything."

"But I want to . . . I need to."

"The pleasures of sin! Humph!" she grunted. Then she told me *her story*. It was heartbreaking, and after hearing it, I had a new understanding of the woman sitting beside me. Sam had had a hard life. She was the fourth of five children in a poor family. She had three older brothers and a baby sister. Abused by her father and bullied by her brothers, Sam learned to fight. She became belligerent and difficult to manage. When she had just turned seven years old she helped her father load up a bunch of junk to take to the city dump.

After they unloaded, he threw one more thing away . . .her. He drove off leaving her there. She never saw her parents or siblings again. Fostered in three different homes, she was never adopted. At sixteen she ran away to live in the streets. At eighteen she hooked up with a hoodlum and drug pusher who pimped her out under a false name. Every day he threatened her with a painful death if she "ratted on him."

The whole time she talked, I was praying, *Oh, God, please bless her and please don't let me look shocked.*

She told me how she got into the satanic cult.

"I ran away from my man and hid from him. After a couple of months, he stopped looking for me, but I had nowhere to go . . . he was my only connection to life." She next joined up with a group of seven homeless people. They provided companionship and to some degree security, although it was a rough group. One night she was approached by two men and a woman who asked if she was hungry. They led her back to a two-story building where they gave her food and offered her shelter for the night. She had never turned down a roof over her head and a free meal.

Over the next few days, no one seemed to be in a hurry to kick her out. Instead, they were friendly and welcoming. She was served breakfast, lunch, and dinner. Snacks were available on a table each day, all day long.

Sam never asked where the food came from, who was paying for it, or why they were so hospitable. She just didn't want it to end. Heavy metal music blared throughout the common room. She had never liked metal music, but people were moving and swaying to its beat while in LSD-induced trances.

The longer she was there, the more friends she made. They assigned duties to her so she could help the group, and she began to feel like she was contributing to her keep. Each night after dinner, they sat around in a circle and discussed national and world affairs. One man in particular sat beside her each evening. He seemed to show some interest in her. She thought he liked her. For the first time, Sam felt a real connection with people, as if she belonged with them. There was no rejection here, unless you didn't obey the leader.

The leader spoke more often than others in those evening meetings. He blamed the world's problems on "naïve people of faith." "All wars are religious wars," he said. "We must discredit all religion that imposes restrictions on our natural desires!" He wasn't talking only about Christianity but *any* faith. "It's *their* belief systems that keeps the world in turmoil," he said. Then one night, he referred to their group as "Satanists who oppose religious morality." Sam was uncomfortable with that term, but she didn't want to go through the ostracism she had seen other members go through for lack of cooperation. She certainly didn't want to lose her meal ticket.

She was ordered to go out and do whatever was necessary to recruit new members. "That's how I met Melanie. But I've had enough of that! When I looked at that sweet girl with her baby, I realized how evil I had become. My life is bad enough, I don't want to do those things anymore. Now you know . . . I don't think God would want anything to do with me."

I reminded her of the woman at the well in John 4. Sam remembered the passage. "This woman was an outcast, trying to avoid people, especially religious people," I said. "She was used and abused too. But then she met Christ, and in that meeting her doubts and questions were answered and she received new life. Even the townspeople were impressed by the change in her life and came out to meet Christ themselves."

It was about 11:30 that evening, and a lull finally crept into the conversation. Quietly, calmly, yet deliberately she said, "I think I want that too."

"What's that? *What* do you want?"

"I want what you've got."

"It's not a thing, Sam. It's a person. Jesus Christ."

"Okay, I want the Jesus you've got."

I didn't want to overreact and scare her away, but every cell in my body was jumping up and down with joy! If you can imagine 37 trillion little guys (the cells in my body) jumping up and down celebrating, shouting, and waving their arms, that's what was going on inside me. Somehow I think they reflect the celebration that was taking place among angels in heaven.

"Sam, are you sure? I mean do you *really* want to turn from Satan to Christ?"

"Yes."

"It's a completely opposite direction from the life you've been living." It almost sounded as if I was trying to talk her out of it, but she needed to understand it meant change. She couldn't live as a *Christian Satanist*. She had to leave the old life.

"I know."

I put my arm around her shoulder, and this hardened woman softened and started crying. She took a tissue from the box on my desk. "I haven't cried in a long time," she said.

Inside that tough exterior, Sam was a hurt little girl who had been robbed of her childhood, her parents, everything most people hold dear and precious in their lives. I was blessed in so many ways that Sam was deprived of. Since that night, I've appreciated those blessings more.

I couldn't imagine the pain, disappointment, and heartbreak this woman must have experienced over the years. But now, all the pent-up emotions were released. First, there were watery eyes, then tears down her cheeks and eventually sobbing as she bent over holding her head in her hands. It was as if a dam that had been feeling pressure against it for so many years finally gave way and a river of emotions poured out. I reached over, took her hands in mine, and asked if I could pray with her. She nodded, "Maybe He will listen to *you.*"

"I know He will." So, I prayed with her and asked the Lord to strengthen her as she made this commitment.

"Sam, Jesus Christ can forgive you of everything in your past and give you the strength to live for Him from this point on."

"How . . . how . . . can I know that?"

"Because He said so and He is—"

"He is truth. Right, I get that. The devil is a liar and God is truth. There *is* a devil, there **must be** a God . . . and He tells the truth. Right?"

I nodded, "Yes."

We had talked about baptism, a picture of the death, burial, and resurrection of Jesus. It represents our *own death to self and coming of new life*, wiping out the past and living for the future. I put my hand on her shoulder and asked, "Will you let me baptize you?"

"Yes."

I led her to the back of the sanctuary where the baptismal changing rooms were. I showed her where the baptismal gowns and towels were and told her I would meet her in the baptistery. In the minister's room, I put on the baptismal boots, which were really chest-high fishing waders. As I walked into the water I could feel the cold penetrate through the rubber boots and I wondered, "Does she know what she's getting into? Will she stay with it? What if she backs out at this moment and leaves?"

She didn't back out.

I watched her as she stepped down into the baptistery, and I was gratified that I didn't see a hardened, world-wizened cynic but rather a humbled, penitent sinner seeking forgiveness. At midnight, I baptized her into Christ, and at 12:01 AM that Sunday morning, the first day of the week, Sam became a *new creature* in Christ!

As we walked back toward my office I asked her, "Sam, do we need to put you up tonight?"

"Naw . . . with your wife, three boys, Melanie, and her baby, you've got enough people. I've got money to get a place. I'll be all right." Then she added, "What time does church start?"

I smiled.

Sunday morning Sam walked into our church building looking completely different. She had stopped at a Walmart Supercenter after leaving me the night before and was now wearing a dress, sandals, and . . . earrings! I could tell she felt awkward, but I wasn't sure if it was because of the clothes or because she was in a church building. She must have wondered whether or not "church people" would accept her. However, our people had always been friendly and welcoming to visitors. Sam was impressed with the genuineness of their faith. I had a feeling that if she did see a counterfeit, she would take it upon herself to expose it.

One Sunday, two weeks later, an adult Bible study teacher came to me with a worried look. "Randy, are you sure about this woman Sam?"

"Why do you ask?"

"Because this morning's lesson was about Jonah and the great fish. After class she came up to me and asked, 'Do you believe that?'"

"What did you say?"

"Well, I said, 'Of course I believe it!' And she said, 'I just wanted to know if *you* believe it.' Then she walked out."

I laughed. "Well, that's Sam! You answered her right. She's okay."

After a few more weeks Sam called to tell me she was returning to New York. There was "business" there she needed to take care of. She promised to keep in touch. A month later, she called and told me she had connected with a Catholic priest and the two of them were going through the parks of New York and destroying satanic altars where dogs, cats, and other animals were sacrificed in satanic rituals.

"Sam," I said, "be careful! This is can be a *dangerous thing* you're doing."

"I know," she said, "but if anything like that happens I'm okay now . . . right? I'm a believer."

For the first few months I heard from Sam regularly. Each time she reaffirmed her faith in Christ and told me of her new adventures. They were stories I think Hollywood would like to get ahold of.

As time passed, the phone calls came less often. I think she was becoming more and more independent. She had joined a Bible study group and found support with them. I haven't heard from Sam in several years now but pray she is well and serving the Lord.

Melanie? That Sunday morning our benevolence committee met with Melanie, and that afternoon they helped her find a place to stay. Our church paid the first month's rent while a couple of the ladies prepared meals and provided childcare for her baby. The church leadership set up an additional benevolent fund that the senior minister could access and also established an account at a nearby hotel I could refer displaced people to. The restrictions here were simply no more than three nights and no long distance phone calls.

Before the first month was up, Melanie had decided to go back to Ohio. A couple of ladies sat with her, one holding her hand and the other an arm around her shoulder, while she called her parents, who were relieved to hear from her. They couldn't wait to see the baby, and her father asked for directions to her rental apartment so he could come for her. "We'll help you," her father said. "We'll help you and Stevie."

*****

Sam demonstrates for us the need for integrity in *both* the ministry and the congregation. That integrity is more than just what you believe, more than believing the right things; it is also how that belief translates into your actions and attitudes. Blatant hypocrisy stands out a mile away, while inner hypocrisy is less obvious until tested.

In their dress and conversation, the priest and Levite in the story of the Good Samaritan *looked* like religious people but when tested proved to be otherwise. Christianity is more than knowing Scripture (Sam proved that) and more than faithfully attending church (I'm afraid *I* proved that.) It's not just knowing Scripture; its *living* it out. It's not just attending church; it's *being* the church. It's not just knowing about Jesus; it's *knowing Him.*

What I Learned

1. I learned many homeless and destitute people are the result of circumstances beyond their control or because of poor decisions.

2. I learned that immaturity and weak values contribute to poor decisions.

3. I learned that EVERYONE needs a helping hand occasionally.

4. I learned to appreciate church members' confidence in the credibility of ministry.

5. I learned to recognize the devil "walks about like a roaring lion seeking to devour people." (I Pete 5:8)

6. I learned to back up my sermons with action.

7. I learned to be sensitive to the leading of the Holy Spirit.

8. I learned to repent every time God brings conviction to my heart.

9. I learned even "evil" people can be converted by God.

10. I learned to consider the power of the evil one. (Jude 1:9)

11. I learned the Bible speaks to people where I fail.

12. I learned hypocrisy comes easy but integrity requires faithfulness.

Leadership Application

1. Read Matthew 16. Research commentaries to determine the significance of the background and setting of Jesus' question, "Who do you say I am?"

   a. Where or when are we challenged to declare faith in Christ?

2. According to pewresearch.org, "As marriage rates have fallen, the number of adults in cohabiting relationships has continued to climb, reaching about 18 million in 2016. This is up 29% since 2007."[1]

   b. Research: What reasons do people give for cohabiting?

   c. How does the Bible address these reasons?

   d. How should cohabitation be addressed from the pulpit in a sermon?

   e. How should church leadership respond to cohabiting couples in the membership?

   f. In the church you attend, how many cohabiting couples are there?

---

[1] Renee Stepler, "Number of U.S. adults cohabiting with a partner continues to rise, especially among those 50 and older," *Pew Research Center*, April 6, 2017, https://www.pewresearch.org/fact-tank/2017/04/06/number-of-u-s-adults-cohabiting-with-a-partner-continues-to-rise-especially-among-those-50-and-older/.

g. How many parents with cohabiting children are in your church?

    a. How do they view their children's cohabitation?

h. Should cohabiting couples be allowed to teach in the church?

i. What policy does the church you attend have in regard to cohabiting couples?

j. What advice can you offer to someone like Melanie who is looking for relationship at any cost?

k. What, if any, policy does your church have regarding babies born to single mothers? Do they shun the birth of these children? Or do they celebrate their birth?

    a. What do you think would be a good approach?

3. What guidelines does your church have regarding benevolence?

a. What percentage of the church's budget is dedicated to benevolence?

b. Who administers that budget and how?

c. How do you distinguish someone who has a genuine need for help from someone soliciting to perpetuate a pernicious lifestyle (e.g. someone looking to secure drugs rather than food or housing)?

d. Does your church restrict benevolence aid to certain needs? What are they (food, housing, medicine)?

e. Contact three other churches, small (less than 100 members), medium (100 to 300 members), and large (over 300 members), and ask the percentage and administrator of the benevolence budget.

    a. On average, how many calls or requests do they receive each month?

    b. What role, if any, does the minister play in meeting benevolent requests?

4. When does your minister begin sermon preparation?

    a. How many hours each week are dedicated to preparing the sermon?

5. How does your church equip members to compassionate needs?

6. Begin a study of Jesus. Did He help/heal everyone with a need?

    a. It appears Jesus had two principles: (1) to confirm His claim as the Son of God (miracles) and (2) to facilitate people who wanted to follow Him (feeding of the 5,000, "you feed them").

7. Suppose your city builds a homeless center and asks for help or support. Are there standards you would expect (regarding matters such as cohabiting) before providing financial assistance?

8. Research: Why do people join cults?

9. How would you approach a Satanist like Sam? Make a brief outline of your points.

10. How would you prepare the church congregation for confrontation about their faith in Christ?

11. What problems do you think a person would have in leaving a cult?

a. How would you address those problems?

12. What aftercare would you recommend for someone who has just left a cult?

b. How would you protect yourself from callousness? How would you keep your heart tender?

The Greatest Resource
in the Church

2

"Preacher, would you leave me your books when you die?"

I was surprised at that request, for a couple of reasons. First, Betty was nearly twenty years *older* than I. And second, Betty Tims was not known to have an "open" mind.

I started a new ministry in Rochester, Virginia. Betty and other church members had volunteered to help set up the office. Betty walked around my office scrutinizing the bookcases I had just loaded up.

My personal library contained a variety of books. In addition to commentaries and reference books, there were business books, motivational books, books written by various professional coaches, books from authors in the Reformation and Restoration movements as well as books from religious authors outside our particular branch of Christianity.

I was trying follow her question, when she added, "You certainly have a lot of books from other churches." *Then* I understood what she was getting at. Betty was a staunch member of a NON-denominational church which had a strong, doctrinal stance. Many people in that area were convinced *any* church *other than their* church was the *wrong* church. Some actually thought of other churches as competitors for members and spent much of their time and resources trying to win each other to their own brand of faith. Betty didn't want her preacher being influenced by outside doctrines.

"Well, Betty," I said, "I'm just practicing what the Bible says."

"What's that?"

"Prove all things, hold fast to that which is good." (In those days the KJV was the most popular Bible translation.)

"That's in the Bible? Where?"

"1 Thessalonians 5:21."

Betty thought for a few moments and then asked, "Well, *will* you leave me your books when you die?"

"I'll probably leave them with my sons. Why? What would *you* do with them?"

"I'll burn them."

I smiled because even though Betty sometimes had a hard edge to her personality, I knew there were other times she could be a very sweet, considerate person as shown in the following account.

*****

The Rochester church was a small congregation with an average attendance of about fifty, and other than myself (the preacher), Betty was the most active member. She taught the ladies' Sunday school class, led the Friday ladies' home Bible study, and spearheaded practically every church fellowship dinner we offered.

As a registered nurse, Betty was accustomed to hard work, difficult people, and irregular hours. Often she would work three or four consecutive days of twelve-hour shifts. Since she had no children and her husband also worked erratic hours, she would volunteer to substitute for others on hospital staff. Betty was not a stranger to responsibility or hard work. I really think she thrived on it.

Opinionated people like Betty are disappointed by many things, but her greatest disappointment was that her husband, Earl, would not attend church with her. Earl was a tough retired coal operator who had supervised scores of hardworking miners and was just as strongly opinionated as his wife. However, they were not agreed about the *need* for church.

Betty talked to me often about her husband. "He's a good man," she would say, "but the Lord is just not in his life. When I ask him to come to worship with me, he says he gets enough religion watching preachers on television." She confessed that she felt somewhat awkward attending without her husband sitting beside her in the pew, but I never doubted that she was genuinely concerned for his soul.

"Watching preachers on television is not church!" she would say. And indeed, it is not. Like Betty, I've been baffled by the number of people who profess faith in Christ yet do not participate in His body, the church.

I once met a man who was pleased to discover that I was a minister. He smiled from ear to ear, put his hand on my shoulder, and said, "I'm really glad to hear that! It's good to know a preacher." I asked him where he went to church, and he said, "Oh, I don't go to a church. I practice John 13:34–35."

Stunned that he would be glad I was a preacher and yet not attend church himself, I couldn't remember what John 13:34–35 said. The reference was familiar, but at the moment, I couldn't recall the verse. "I know the address but can't remember the verse. What is it?"

"A new command I give you, love one another. By this all men will know you are my disciples if you love one another." Then he added, "That's what *I* live by."

"That's great!" I said. "But what do you do with the *rest* of the Bible?"

"What do you mean?"

"Well, you're right that love is essential to the Christian life, but the rest of the Bible tells us how to do that. We have privileges, responsibilities, and duties. That's why the book of Acts emphasizes that the church *gathered* together regularly. Those church members didn't just hear a sermon; they participated in communion, encouraged one another, organized opportunities for service, and often discovered there were people in their fellowship with needs. Without the gathering, they wouldn't have known about the needs. You see, God blesses you so *you* can bless others. That's primarily done through the church. 'Therefore, as we have opportunity, let us do good to all people, *especially* to those who belong to the family of believers.'[2]

The look on my new friend's face told me he was surprised by my objection.

"In fact, the body of Christ is not as effective as it could be because you're not there participating, contributing *your* talents and resources, praising and uplifting God. You're holding out! Hebrews 10:24–25 says, 'And let us consider how we may spur one another on toward love and good deeds, not giving up meeting together, as some are in the habit of doing, but encouraging one another—and all the more as you see the Day approaching.'"

He looked around to see if anyone was listening, maybe wondering if someone would come by and rescue him.

I went on, "The Apostle Paul described our *collective* worship as a powerful witness: 'But if an unbeliever or an inquirer comes in while everyone is prophesying, they are convicted of sin and are brought under judgment by all, as the secrets of their hearts are laid bare. So they will fall down and worship God, exclaiming, "God is really among you!"'[3] By your absence from church worship, you're not participating in that witness.

Now he gave me a wry look, as if annoyed.

---

[2] Galatians 6:10
[3] 1 Corinthians 14:24–25

"Another fact," I said, "almost everything the Bible has to say to the individual Christian is said in the context of the local church. Romans, 1 and 2 Corinthians, Ephesians, Philippians, and more were written to local churches and proclaimed to the gathering of their members. Truth is, if you're not participating in a local church, whatever else it may be, it is not *biblical* Christianity."

I recalled the story told of Chicago minister D. L. Moody's visiting a man one cold January evening and inviting him to attend church. "I can be a Christian without a church!" the man insisted. Moody stood, walked over to the fireplace, took the tongs, grabbed a live coal, and set it on the hearth without saying a word. Moody then sat back down and stared at the coal. The man followed Moody's gaze, and the two of them watched the coal in silence. The red hot coal turned gray and then within a few moments to black. The man looked at Moody and said, "I understand your point. When you removed that coal from the the the fire, you removed it from the source of heat and it died."

By now my new friend had become impatient. "Humph!" He turned and started talking to someone else. I think I might have pressed the issue a little too much.

A little over a year later, Earl was diagnosed with cancer. After he went through multiple treatments involving radiation and chemotherapy, he began wondering, what happens when people die? Is that it? Do they just cease to exist? Am I *more* than flesh and blood? For several weeks I visited the Tims' home praying and sharing scriptures with him. There were times he phoned me to ask questions about death and, in particular, the afterlife.

One of the most thought-provoking illustrations I have heard on this subject was given by Don DeWelt, author and former professor at Ozark Bible College (now Ozark University). Don said you can go to any mortuary and look at any corpse. That corpse will have eyes to see, but they cannot see. Ears to hear that cannot hear. A mouth to speak that cannot speak. Why? Physically, everything is there. What's missing?

What's missing is the human spirit that God placed within us when we were conceived.

The Bible says, "The body without the spirit is dead" (James 2:26) and "the dust returns to the ground it came from, and the spirit returns to God who gave it" (Ecclesiastes 12:7).

Don would go on to explain, "You see with your spirit *through* your eyes. You hear with your spirit *through* your ears. You speak with your spirit *through* your lips."

With this explanation, Earl began to understand that the body wears out but the spirit lives on.

After months of treatment and therapy, it became clear Earl would not survive this cancer. However, during that time, he became a believer in God, and in the Word of God; he confessed faith in Jesus Christ and was baptized. This newfound faith gave both Betty and Earl a sense of peace before his passing. After his funeral, Betty continued her work for the Lord and seemed more congenial than before. That congeniality was evidenced in what happened a few short weeks after Earl's passing.

*****

After Earl's death, Betty struggled with loneliness. Her house had never felt so empty before. Even though Earl would go to work or go to take care of some chore, leaving her alone in their large home, she never felt lonely knowing he would return. But this was different. She would not see him again until the Lord came back or she went to be with him in heaven, whichever came first.

For the first week, Betty tried to fend off the loneliness by staying busy attending to "church work." That plan worked well through the days, but evenings were more difficult. Most evenings she would sit on the couch studying her lesson material or watching TV. At least the television would give the sound of voices throughout the house. When she became bored with television, she would make cookies or bake a cake that she could take to a shut-in the next day, or she would sit at the kitchen table and write notes of encouragement to church members. She was determined not to let anyone see her grieve, lest they think she didn't have enough faith to handle her loss. For as long as people at church had known her, Betty presented herself as a model of faith and strength. Now, however, she was struggling. So she buried her anguish deep within her until the private moments at night when she could release it to the Lord and let the tears flow.

Betty leaned forward, stretched her arms out across the table and clasped her hands in prayer. "O Lord, *dear Lord*…I don't know what to do. I have never felt so lost as I do now. Help me please," she prayed. She remembered a statement in a devotional guide she read weeks earlier, "God NEVER wastes a tear." She repeated that statement over and over in her mind. Leaning back in her chair now she said out loud, "I wonder what God will do with *these* tears."

*****

While her mother looked the other way, Ellie looked into the car's mirror at her left temple. There was an open cut above her eye, and the whole side of her face was beginning to darken. She licked at the left side of her busted lip and pulled her hair over the right side of her face so her mother wouldn't see her tears. Holding the steering wheel with her left arm, she reached over and massaged her left shoulder. She gripped the wheel with both hands and leaned forward to straighten her back. Every part of her body was aching. She chanced a sideways glance at her mother, who was passively staring out the passenger window, not really focusing on anything but seemingly deep in thought. Ellie could sense the fear from her mother's posture but decided not to disturb her. There was no conversation between the two of them. Just silence.

In the back seat were two large garbage bags filled with her mother's belongings. This wasn't all of her possessions, but they would have to get the rest later. For now, she had to find a place for her mother, because she wasn't safe at home.

Ellie's home was a two-bedroom rental trailer up a lonely hollow nestled between the mountains, nearly five miles from the church building. She and her husband Jimmy had been married almost a year and at the beginning had high hopes of getting their own place, raising children, and planting a garden in the backyard. Ellie's father had deserted them twelve years earlier, and it had just been she and her mother until Jimmy came into their lives. In his proposal, Jimmy had offered to take care of them both. "Her Social Security will help with the bills, and we'll get a place that much quicker," he reasoned. However, her mother's check was barely enough to pay for her medicine.

Jimmy was a hot-tempered and easily agitated garage mechanic who was always under pressure. His boss was taking in more repairs than they could keep up with, and when Jimmy fell behind, he threated to replace him. Every day he endured the hateful demands of customers and antagonism from his boss. Jimmy was a walking time bomb ready to explode. To make matters worse, he drank a lot, and when he was drunk he became belligerent. This particular evening he had stopped at a roadside bar to relax but started drinking heavily. He came home drunk, used foul language, and complained about everything. He didn't like the dinner Ellie had prepared, she hadn't washed the shirt he wanted to wear, and they had no privacy because Ellie's mother was always there.

When Ellie stood up to speak for her mother, Jimmy struck her. Immediately Ellie's mother hurried to intervene, and Jimmy drew his arm back to swing at *her*. Ellie quickly jumped in front of her mother and absorbed the blow. This blow to the left side of her face sent her staggering across the room and into the kitchen table. She hit the table on her side, which she was sure broke one of her ribs. The room grew dark around her as she started to lose consciousness. As if far away, she could hear her mother screaming, "Jimmy! Jimmy, stop! You'll kill her!" Ellie, her resolve strengthening at her mother's shrieks, stood and looked at Jimmy, who was standing across the room with a look of bewilderment on his face. His mouth opened as he looked back at her, but no words came out.

Thinking she may have a broken rib, Ellie pressed her arm tightly against her side and hobbled to her mother. She glared at Jimmy, daring him to make a move toward them, then took her mother's arm, pulled her into the nearest bedroom, and slammed the door behind them. In a final act she made the door's lock click as loudly as she could.

A few moments later, Ellie heard the door of the trailer slam as Jimmy stormed out to cool off. Then she hurried into the kitchen, grabbed a couple of kitchen garbage bags, and started stuffing her mother's clothes into them. They got into the car, and Ellie put the '92 Dodge Colt into first gear and peeled out, throwing dirt and gravel at the trailer they had called home for the past eight months.

Finally, her mother was the first to speak. "Where are we going? What are we going to do?"

"Mom, I've got to find a place for you. It's not safe at home."

At this, her mother began to panic, "Where?! Where are you taking me? *Where* can we go?"

Ellie had no idea. She was willing to go back to the trailer and reason with Jimmy after he had sobered up. Maybe they could get help for his drinking. But she could not take her mother back. She **would not** take her back! But where would she take her? They had no family members to turn to, and she didn't know anyone else in their area.

Ellie searched her mind for people they knew, then finally off in the distance she could see the steeple of a church building they had visited a couple of times. She remembered how a "nice lady" there had welcomed them. They had tried to attend incognito, but this woman wouldn't let them escape after the service. She was very friendly and outgoing. Ellie tried to remember the name. *Barbara? . . . No, it was Betty! She lived on the hill near the church. She's the only one I can think of to ask.*

*****

35

Betty opened the door to two women standing on her porch. One younger, one older. She acknowledged the older lady but couldn't keep from looking back at the younger one. Her clothes were disheveled and her hair was mussed up. Betty had often triaged patients in the local hospital emergency room, so she focused on the black eye with a cut over the eyebrow. Since the highway ran by her house, she instantly thought the two had been in a car wreck and without hesitation pulled the younger one inside.

"Oh, my goodness," Betty said, "we've got to treat that wound immediately." She led them to the bathroom, then rushed to the kitchen for an ice pack. She filled it up with crushed ice and put it in Ellie's hand and then had Ellie hold the pack on her left temple while she examined the cut over her eye. She decided stitches were not necessary and put a couple of butterfly bandages across it. As she was tending to the younger woman, the older woman explained what happened.

Ellie began to sob. "I don't know what I'm going to do. I can't take Mom back there. He resents her being in the trailer with us. Where can we go? Do you know *any* place? My mom has a touch of forgetfulness. She forgets to take her medicine, and she gets bad off. Do you know *anyone* who can help us?"

"We should call the police!" Betty demanded.

"Oh no! I don't want to put Jimmy in jail. He'll be all right. He just has so much pressure on him. He's not like this all the time. We just need something temporary till we can get a place."

Betty looked at Ellie and then the mother, all the while her mind was searching for answers. She knew in their small community there was no shelter or rescue station for them. And they couldn't go back to the trailer where Jimmy could return anytime even drunker and angrier than before.

"Your mom can stay here with me. I'm a nurse, so I can administer her medications . . . In fact, you both stay here. You can help me take care of her."

At first, Ellie and her mother didn't know whether to believe Betty. They hesitated to respond.

Betty sensed their apprehension. "Look, let's just plan on a week. That will give you time to decide what you're going to do and search for a place to house your mother."

Ellie and her mother looked at each other and almost simultaneously, with a breath of relief, said, "Thank you so much." Then Betty led them to a guest room, gave them a few minutes to get cleaned up, and brought towels and a set of her own clothes for each of them to change into. An hour later they were sitting around the kitchen table eating grilled cheese sandwiches while Betty told them about herself and laid down expectations she had of them. Ellie and her mother agreed, and all three declared it a night.

Early the next morning, Betty woke up to find the two women sitting at the kitchen table waiting for her. They sheepishly smiled, greeted her, and sat quietly and patiently waiting for the "next shoe to drop." The silence was awkward and uncomfortable for Betty. She turned toward them, put her hands on her hips, and said, "Now look, we're in this together. We can help each other out. You can wash your clothes; you can help yourself to the food in the refrigerator and cabinets. Then you can clean up your room and help me keep this house clean. Got it?"

"Yes ma'am," they both responded.

Betty then told them her schedule for the day and how they could help. Somehow, having these responsibilities divvied out made each of them feel better. Then, they went to work.

Over the next few days, Ellie went back to the trailer to gather her and her mother's belongings. She waited till she knew Jimmy had gone to work. After four trips, she said goodbye to the trailer that had been her home, then started looking for a place that could house her mother. A week went by with no success.

One morning while gathered for breakfast, Betty asked how the search was going. Ellie was afraid that Betty had reached the end of her patience with them.

"Not very good," she answered. "Nobody knows where we can go." Ellie gave a quick glance at her mother, and Betty understood. It would be difficult to find a place for her mother, a woman on heavy medications.

"Then you'll stay here until you do."

Another sigh of relief from the two women.

Three months later, a spirit of harmony covered the home as they grew more acquainted. They genuinely seemed to like each other. Ellie asked if she and her mother could plant a garden in the yard behind the house. "We'll tend to it. It won't be a burden on you."

"Absolutely!" Betty smiled. "I've always wanted a garden, but you know nurses have crazy schedules, and then my husband got sick . . . I never got around to planting one. But I think it would be wonderful! Let's do it!"

Betty assumed they were talking about a few flowers, but she learned later they had planted tomatoes, potatoes, green beans, lettuce, cabbage, sugar snap peas (her favorite), and some flowers. It turned out Ellie and her mother were accustomed to gardening and canning vegetables.

One evening, nearly four months later, the three of them were sitting around the kitchen table enjoying a meal of pork chops, peas, and boiled potatoes when someone knocked at the door. Betty hadn't said anything, but she fully expected Jimmy to eventually show up. She had thought about an encounter often since that first night and had prepared for his coming. Maybe he was knocking at her door now. She stood, steeled herself, straightened her clothes, and walked resolutely to the front door.

When she opened the door she was surprised to find an elderly woman staring directly into her eyes. Neither of them said anything at first, they just stood there gawking at each other. Betty gauged her to be in her late seventies. She was wearing a heavy, threadbare cable knit sweater, and a beat-up suitcase stood by her side. *Now what?!* Betty thought to herself.

Betty spoke first. "Can I help you?"

The woman said, "I hear you take in women with no place to go."

"Who told you *that?!*"

"The preacher at the church around the curve." She pointed to Betty's right, the general direction where the Rochester Church building stood.

"Here we go again," Betty said under her breath. Then louder to the woman on her porch, "Well, why don't you come in and tell me about it." She stepped onto the porch, picked up the suitcase, and led the woman in to meet the other two ladies in her kitchen.

Betty did, in fact, allow the woman to stay. She too found ways she could help. However, that was not the end of it. These stories were repeated again and again. Within the year, another woman had shown up on Betty's porch. Then another. She applied for and received a license to operate a home for women. Her nursing degree came in handy as she ministered to each of them. Her husband's life insurance was generous and more than provided for her needs. She had a friend at the hospital who helped her find grants and monies to provide medical care for the impoverished. When any of these ladies became ill, each of the other women would take turns providing care and comfort.

Betty conducted Bible studies with them, teaching them about Jesus. Most of them received Christ as Savior, and all of those who were able attended church with her.

As their number grew, Betty made adjustments to the house. She hired a carpenter to install petitions, dividing her living room into two bedrooms that would house more women, and she added a bathroom at each end of the house. Not long after that, Betty bought a used mobile home, parked it in the backyard, and moved into it herself! "A woman's got to have some privacy now and then," she said. Ellie began taking more and more responsibility for managing the home, giving Betty more free time than she needed, so she went back to her "church work."

Ellie never saw or heard from Jimmy again. When she drove by the trailer, there were new occupants who told her Jimmy had lost his job and moved out of state. They didn't know where. Ellie was saddened by that news because she had hoped Jimmy could get things together in his life and abstain from alcohol. She prayed that someone, somewhere would influence him for Christ. After two more months of not hearing from him, an attorney friend of Betty's recommended she file for an annulment of the marriage.

When word got out that Betty was taking these women into her home, church members started baking cookies and cakes, even volunteering to make meals or do things around the house. However, while Betty and her guests enjoyed and appreciated those contributions, for the most part the "facility" had become self-sufficient. By the time Betty went to the Lord in 1993, twelve women had taken up residence in The Manor Rest Home. Finding so much grace in the hearts of these women, Betty also founded Rochester Day Care Center, where single working mothers were provided childcare on a cost-only basis.

After more than forty-five years, I still look back with gratitude for Betty's life and ministry. In a small town she made a huge impact. In the church she made an impact. All it took was one individual to kickstart the church into a wonderful compassion ministry. Those impacts didn't come about through a rigid, formal "religiosity," but rather from a big heart made tender by the love of Christ.

What I Learned

- I learned that strong women should be appreciated and their energies channeled into ministries.

- I learned every local church is made up of legalistic, liberal, and indifferent people as well as people like Betty. My purpose was to help them understand God's Word.

- I learned the best "ministers" are not necessarily on the platform but in the congregation.

- I learned the importance of addressing domestic abuse often from the pulpit.

- I learned to teach the church anger management and conflict resolution skills from the Bible.

Leadership Application

1. Look at your local church. What percent would you guess is liberal, legalistic, or indifferent?

2. How many people in your circle of acquaintances substitute TV preachers for church services?

3. What are the advantages of a local church over TV religion?

4. Investigate domestic abuse in your community. How many cases have there been in the last twelve months?

5. What signs indicate domestic abuse?

6. Does your church have a ministry to victims of domestic abuse?

7. In your view, what is the best way to address this issue in the church?

8. Investigate: what are the steps to report domestic abuse?

9. What is the most effective way to teach conflict resolution in church?

10. How does your church minister to the elderly? To young marrieds?

How Long Must I Put Up with Them?

3

It was a solemn occasion, surreal, even inspirational. They'd had a mountaintop experience and were on a "spiritual high," but spiritual highs typically don't last long, and this one was no exception. Jesus and his three companions descended the mountain to a commotion below. First, they heard the clamor, and then, as they drew closer, they could see the source. From their vantage point they could see a cluster of people at the base of the mountain pressing in toward the center. In the middle of that cluster were the other disciples. The "inner circle," Peter, James, and John, had accompanied Jesus up the mountain, leaving the other nine behind to tend to the people.

The trio with Jesus was ecstatic having seen Him transfigured before their eyes. Earlier, they had all seen Him walk on water. Now, Jesus, on the mountaintop, had pulled back the veil of His humanity and allowed them to see His glory; "His face shone like the sun, and his clothes became as white as the light" (Matthew 17:2). The brightness of Jesus' face and clothing was blinding. They knelt before Him and stretched out their hands, shielding their eyes. Appearing with Jesus on each side were Moses and Elijah, great patriarchs of the faith.

Now, they were returning to the others. As they descended, Jesus told the three disciples, "Don't tell anyone what you have seen, until the Son of Man has been raised from the dead" (Matthew 17:9). They must have looked at each other, puzzled. Why not? How could they keep this experience to themselves? How could they stop themselves from shouting it to everyone they met? Why *wouldn't* they . . . other than because Jesus told them not to? It must have been difficult to withhold this experience from the others. Later, John would write, "The Word became flesh and made his dwelling among us. We have seen his glory, the glory of the one and only Son, who came from the Father, full of grace and truth" (John 1:14). And Peter recalled, "we were eyewitnesses of his majesty. He received honor and glory from God the Father when the voice came to him from the Majestic Glory, saying, 'This is my Son, whom I love; with him I am well pleased.' We ourselves heard this voice that came from heaven when we were with him on the sacred mountain" (2 Peter 1:16–18).

As they approached the crowd, a man ran up and knelt before Jesus, pleading with Him to help his son:

"Lord, have mercy on my son," he said. "He has seizures and is suffering greatly. He often falls into the fire or into the water. I brought him to your disciples, but they could not heal him."

"You unbelieving and perverse generation," Jesus replied, "how long shall I stay with you? *How long shall I put up with you?* Bring the boy here to me." Jesus rebuked the demon and it came out of the boy, and he was healed at that moment. (Matthew 17:15–18, author's emphasis)

"How long shall I put up with you?" That's the part where I smile. It's not a particularly humorous event, given the desperation of the father and the affliction of the son, but I find it gratifying that Jesus knew the challenge of working with difficult people. You see, the disciples disappointed Jesus because he had already given them the authority and power to heal the young man (Matthew 10:1).

It is not easy to imagine Jesus experiencing *any* degree of frustration, in that even the wind and the waves were in his control (Matthew 8:27), yet the Bible does tell us Jesus was tempted "in every way, just as we are—yet he did not sin" (Hebrews 4:15).

Turn back a few chapters and notice the difficulties that led to his lament. In chapter 14, thousands were following Jesus, many of them sick, infirm, crippled, blind, and desperate. The heart of God in Jesus was touched by their infirmities (Hebrews 4:15). Verse 14 tells us, "When Jesus landed and saw a large crowd, he had compassion on them and healed their sick." But as the day wore on, the disciples worried how they would accommodate such a crowd:

"Send the crowds away, so they can go to the villages and buy themselves some food."
Jesus replied, "They do not need to go away. *You* give them something to eat." (vv. 15–16, author's emphasis)

They were finding problems, not solutions.

Jesus had come to seek and to save the lost (John 10:10), but the disciples would have rejected them. He had come to teach them the Word of God, yet the disciples would have sent them away. Jesus knew what it was to put up with people who had different agendas and goals for the congregation than He had, people who were overly practical and easily inconvenienced or irritated.

Just after this, still in chapter 14, was when Jesus walked on water. As He approached the disciples' boat, Peter called out, "Lord, if it's you . . . tell me to come to you on the water" (v. 28). Jesus said, "Come." Peter stepped out of the boat and momentarily was standing on water—not on a solid surface, but water! Then, as he started walking, he took his eyes off Jesus and focused on the wind and the waves. He lost sight of his goal to reach Jesus and started sinking. "Lord, save me!" he cried (v. 30).

Jesus reached out His hand and caught him. "You of little faith," He said, "why did you doubt?" (vv. 30–31). Jesus knew what it was to put up with people of little faith, weak faith.

In chapter 15, the Pharisees criticized the disciples because they didn't follow the traditions of the elders (v. 3). Jesus rebuked them for their callousness and disobedience to a command of God. He called them hypocrites (v. 7). Then, in verse 12, the disciples approached Jesus concerned that He had "offended" the Pharisees. Jesus knew what it was to put up with people who were worried about offending the very people who had threatened their ministry. The disciples were willing to compromise their message to avoid trouble.

Later in that same chapter, a Canaanite woman came to Jesus crying out, "Lord, Son of David, have mercy on me! My daughter is demon-possessed and suffering terribly" (Matthew 15:22). The disciples came to Jesus and once again urged Him to avoid her: "Send her away, for she keeps crying out after us" (v. 23). Jesus knew what it was to put up with people who were impatient and indifferent to the needs of others.

In chapter 16, Jesus warned His disciples about the false teaching of the Pharisees and Sadducees using the illustration of yeast, implying the teaching of both groups had a corrupting effect. These men missed his point entirely: "They discussed this among themselves and said, 'It is because we didn't bring any bread'" (Matthew 16:7). Jesus knew what it was like to put up with people who were slow to catch on, people who thought materially rather than spiritually.

In Matthew 16:21–23, Jesus explained to His disciples that He would be arrested and killed in Jerusalem. When He did, Peter reacted strongly:

> Peter took him aside and began to rebuke him. "Never, Lord!" he said. "This shall never happen to you!"
> Jesus turned and said to Peter, "Get behind me, Satan! You are a stumbling block to me; you do not have in mind the concerns of God but merely human concerns." (Matthew 16:22–23)

Jesus knew what it was to put up with people who opposed His mission, who were *stumbling blocks.*

Finally, as Peter was euphoric by the transfiguration of Christ, he was doubly astonished by the appearance of Moses and Elijah. Impulsively he felt the need to *do something* to mark the occasion by offering to build three tabernacles, one for each of them. "While he was still speaking, a bright cloud covered them, and a voice from the cloud said, "This is my

Son, whom I love; with him I am well pleased. Listen to him!" (Matthew 17:5). Jesus put up with well-meaning but misguided people.

In the span of just four chapters, we see that Jesus' followers had different goals than He, were weak in faith, were unconcerned about the needs of others, were slow to catch on, and were resistant to the work of God. Jesus must have wondered at times, *Are we on the same team?* Why should we expect anything different from people today? Church members are *still* concerned about their comfort, their time, and their preferences.

Think of it, Jesus chose these men from all those who followed Him. Why not choose men like Samuel or Isaiah or Joshua, whose hearts were in tune with His? Instead He chose hardened, uneducated, obstinate fishermen, tax collectors, and a zealot. Somehow, I think, this must have been a part of the experience of humanity He would take part in: "Because he himself suffered when he was tempted, he is able to help those who are being tempted" (Hebrews 2:18).

Not long ago a young minister was expressing his frustration with a board member. "I like him. He's a sincere worker, but he's impatient, always blurting out in board meetings and challenging leadership decisions. I never know what he's going to say. Sometimes it's embarrassing. He speaks without thinking. He doesn't listen; he just talks."

I said, "Do you know who else was like that? . . . The apostle Peter."

He leaned his head back and opened his mouth in realization. "Ohhh . . . That's true, isn't it!"

If you tried, I imagine you would see in many of your members the characteristics of these disciples. One loud and brash (Peter). One quiet, calm, and devoted (John). One overeager, ready to go at a moment's notice (Simon, the zealot). One who found problems with every proposal (Thomas). One who was always worried about money and questioned cost (Philip). Another who was good at numbers (Matthew the tax collector). And still another who was perhaps just using church connections to advance his own agenda (Judas).

We must remember, Jesus changed the world with *these* men. Judas was lost, but the other disciples preached the gospel and started the church. God inspired them to write most of the New Testament. Who would have guessed that these difficult, uneducated, often quarrelling men could start a movement that would spread across the world or would write a book that would stand for centuries?

How did Jesus change these men? He did not do it by using supernatural power *upon* them. Rather, He lived a *super*-natural life *before* them. He shows us the answer to difficult people, contention, and division is humble servanth`ood.

PARADIGM SHIFT

I can't imagine how the disciples could argue among themselves over who was the greatest (Luke 9:46–48) when the Son of God was in their presence. Yet they did. Jesus then pointed to a child as an example of greatness. It's not easy to teach someone who considers himself superior to his teacher. This child demonstrated the need for gentle humility, a willingness to learn. The disciples needed a paradigm shift and Jesus was the one to bring it about.

The disciples had come to love and respect Jesus. As they travelled with Him, they listened to His teaching, watched the crowds press in upon Him, observed His actions and reactions. Except possibly for Judas, the disciples were convinced He was the Messiah (Luke 9:20). Repeatedly Jesus taught them the truths of God and demonstrated those truths in His own life. However, I think the experience that must have dealt a devastating blow to their subjective pride took place in the upper room as Jesus humbled himself and knelt before them to wash their feet. Peter immediately objected, but Jesus said, "Unless I wash you, you have no part with me" (John 13:8). Peter responded, "Then, Lord . . . not just my feet but my hands and my head as well" (v. 9). Peter had experienced a paradigm shift.

Merriam-Webster defines paradigm shift as "an important change that happens when the usual way of thinking about or doing something is replaced by a new and different way."[1] Has that ever happened to you? It has to me.

Other than Jesus, the man I have come to respect the most in my life is my father. I didn't realize it until after he went to the Lord, but his influence still remains in my heart more than fifty years later.

For several years my father earned a living as a barber, standing on his feet nearly ten hours a day, six days a week. One of my responsibilities as a junior high teenager was to mow the lawn every Saturday. There is one Saturday I will never forget. It was a hot summer day, over ninety degrees, and I was watching a ball game on TV. I was so engrossed in the game, I didn't pay any attention to the time or to my duties. Around 8:30 that evening, Dad walked in. "Whatcha doin'?" he asked.

I kept my eyes focused on the game, not really paying any attention to Dad's presence. "Just watchin' a game," I said. "It's good one."

About ten minutes later I heard the roar of the lawnmower in the front yard and ran to the window to see Dad doing my job. I knew the kind of day he must have had, so I ran outside and stopped him. I shouted over the racket our ancient push mower was making, "Dad, I'll do that. Let *me* have the mower."

"No. I started it, I'll finish it. You sit down right there on the porch. We'll talk when I'm done." He pointed to the front porch, and I walked over to the front steps and sat down. Dad continued to mow.

As the sun began to set and the sky was growing darker, I turned on the porch light so he could see better. At this point, I hoped any positive action from me might be welcome.

I watched him marching back and forth across the lawn. My heart sank and my shame grew with each step he took. Finally, he finished. I

---

[1] "Paradigm shift," *Merriam-Webster.com*, accessed May 1, 2019, https://www.merriam-webster.com/dictionary/paradigm%20shift.

offered to put the mower away, but he insisted on doing it. "Come with me," he said. After securing the door to shed he turned, faced me, then put his arm around my shoulder and said, "Now, let's go in and see if you left me anything to eat from dinner."

After that, Dad never had to cut the grass again while I was there. I had a paradigm shift.

That shift in my attitude didn't come from corporal discipline or privilege denials or threats. It came from a man who was *willing to pay a price* to teach me a lesson.

The real test of a saint is not one's willingness to preach the gospel but one's willingness to do something like washing the disciples' feet—that is, being willing to do those things that seem unimportant in human estimation but count as everything to God.

Oswald Chambers[2]

WE MUST EARN THE RIGHT TO BE HEARD

"We must earn the right to be heard." I'm not sure who first said those words, but they have haunted me throughout my ministry. One summer, my wife and I were visiting Williamsburg, VA when they became even more concrete for me. Walking down the brick sidewalks and road to Colonial Williamsburg, we enjoyed a warm, beautiful, sunny day. The sidewalks as well as the middle of the road were crowded with hundreds of tourists, people of all ages and backgrounds, male and female, who came to delve into America's heritage. There were some had come from rural and urban areas. There were college students, senior citizens, and children.

On one side of the road was Bruton Parish, a 300-year-old Episcopal church. Across the road from the Parish, an unidentified man stood on

---

[2] Taken from *My Utmost for His Highest* by Oswald Chambers, edited by James Reimann, © 1992 by Oswald Chambers Publications Assn., Ltd., and used by permission of Discovery House Publishers, Grand Rapids MI 49501. All rights reserved.

a soapbox elevated two to three feet above the heads of passersby. With a Bible in his left hand, he raised his arm and shook his fist skyward as he bellowed out about sin and repentance. He must have condemned a dozen different sins from his platform.

What interested me was that most people on his side of the road walked around him without paying any attention. Some laughed and mocked, others sneered, yet he droned on. I thought to myself, "Why should he expect any of them to listen to him? They don't know him. He hasn't earned any credibility with them." It occurred to me that ministry is most often built around relationships with credibility.

A recent research poll from Lifeway Research suggested the average pastor's tenure in a local church is 3.6 years. Studies of effective leaders suggest an average tenure of 11.2 to 21.6 years. Trevin Wax suggests that most studies of the average tenure in a local church show the number to be between 5 and 7 years.[3]

When Jesus taught, people listened because He had fed them, healed their sick, and demonstrated the power of the Holy Spirit through His works. They knew He cared. Jesus showed kindness and compassion in spite of persecution by the Pharisees. People were willing to listen to Jesus because they knew that, unlike the Pharisees, He genuinely cared for them. He reserved His harshest words for the hypocritical Pharisees, but when Jesus spoke to the people, He spoke of a better way of living and better way of life. The beatitudes, the Sermon on the Mount, remain the most powerful and beautiful words in history. When Jesus said, "God loves you and I do too," the people believed Him. He had earned the right to be heard.

---

[3] Dr. Franklin Dumond, "Eight Point Eight Two: How long do pastors stay in one church?" *For Every Man* (blog), June 26, 2014, http://www.gbjournal.org/8-82/.

STAY ON HIGH GROUND

As I think back, the most difficult people in my ministry were "ruling" members (who insisted every decision be made with their approval), controlling members (who wanted all the attention of ministry), indifferent members (who were uninvolved and stayed on the fringe), and hyperactive members (who wanted to try every program and project imaginable outside our mission).

Regardless of which type of member may be causing difficulty, it's best to "stay on high ground." At first glance, that expression means don't sink to their level. However, Christ expects more from his followers:

> "You have heard that it was said, 'Eye for eye, and tooth for tooth.' But I tell you, do not resist an evil person. If anyone slaps you on the right cheek, turn to them the other cheek also. And if anyone wants to sue you and take your shirt, hand over your coat as well. If anyone forces you to go one mile, go with them two miles. Give to the one who asks you, and do not turn away from the one who wants to borrow from you.
> "You have heard that it was said, 'Love your neighbor and hate your enemy.' But I tell you, love your enemies and pray for those who persecute you, that you may be children of your Father in heaven. He causes his sun to rise on the evil and the good, and sends rain on the righteous and the unrighteous. If you love those who love you, what reward will you get? Are not even the tax collectors doing that? And if you greet only your own people, what are you doing more than others? Do not even pagans do that? Be perfect, therefore, as your heavenly Father is perfect."
> (Matthew 5:38–48)
>
> Let us not become weary in doing good, for at the proper time we will reap a harvest if we do not give up.
> (Galatians 6:9)

In everything set them an example by doing what is good.
In your teaching show integrity, seriousness and soundness
of speech that cannot be condemned, so that those who
oppose you may be ashamed because they have nothing
bad to say about us. (Titus 2:7–8)

I'm ashamed to say I haven't always done this. However, the times I have followed these directives, I've been glad I did. Three men in particular come to mind. Two had been elders but had not been reelected to office in a church vote weeks before I began ministry. The third had been and still was a deacon. These men were good friends and met together often.

Karl was the oldest, mid-seventies, and of the three seemingly had the strongest personality. He was a tall man with a voice that had an authoritative tone to it. When he spoke, he gave the impression that he knew more and knew better. Having been a smoker for decades, Karl had developed worsening emphysema. It was increasingly difficult for him to breathe, walk for long distances, or climb stairs.

Al, on the other hand, was in relatively good health for a man in his early seventies. He had a quick-thinking mind and could have a sharp edge to his voice that would often be tinged with cynicism.

Nick was a much younger man in his early fifties when I came. Looking at him, you would think he was the picture of health. However, he had a weak heart and had gone through a heart transplant in Texas. His body was not readily accepting the new heart, so he made frequent trips to the cardiologist.

Like Karl, Nick also had a strong personality but would often be very congenial. I discovered, though, you don't want to get on the wrong foot with him. Our youth minister, Kevin, learned this the hard way.

Kevin had been the youth minister for several months by this time. He was an amiable young man who wore a constant smile. Kids liked him, parents liked him, even senior saints liked him. He was easy to get along with, but one day he inadvertently found himself in conflict.

Nick's daughter had married a young man whose family was also deeply connected at the church. After two years of marriage, they went through a difficult divorce, which put a strain on both families as well as the church. One Sunday after worship service, Kevin and his wife were dining at a local restaurant and Nick approached him. "Kevin, I want to thank you for speaking to my daughter this morning. She's uncomfortable at church now, and it did her good to hear a friendly voice."

"Oh, that's all right. I'm glad to do it," Kevin said. "I don't condone what she did, but I still want to be friendly to her." Kevin meant to say, "While I regret no-fault divorce, I know it must have been difficult for her, but she's still our friend and we care for her."

Nick's face turned red immediately, and he became volatile, berating Kevin for "judging his daughter."

He spoke at the same volume, but now his words were infused with anger, "And just who made you god?! You don't know anything about what my daughter went through!" People in the restaurant turned to see what was going on.

Kevin realized how his words must have sounded and apologized. However, Nick wouldn't accept it and stormed off. After that, he took steps to have Kevin disciplined. He contacted me, then contacted the elders to complain. I called him to say how much I regretted that the incident had happened and that Kevin and I had talked. I told him that Kevin was remorseful, "He feels terrible about his words. He understands you were offended, and he's very sorry. One of the goals of ministry is to strengthen marriages. But Nick, he's learned from this." He took that in stride.

The following Sunday, I didn't see Nick or his family at worship, so on Monday I sent a card letting him know we cared about his family and I was keeping them in prayer. One morning a few days later, Nick called me. "I received your note," he said. "Thank you for writing. I think we should meet."

I saw that as a good sign and offered to go to him.

It was not a good sign after all. When I arrived at his home, Nick graciously received me and offered coffee or iced tea. Then he proceeded to transfer his anger from Kevin to *me*. I had shown no concern for his daughter and no intention of disciplining Kevin.

When I realized we weren't going to settle the issue, I thanked him for contacting me, wished him well, and left.

As you can imagine, Nick and Al started visiting other churches. Two weeks later, the minister of a neighboring church called to tell me Al had visited their church and ask whether he should call to welcome him. (He was extending a courtesy to let me know one of our sheep had wandered into the neighbor's flock.) Then he revealed that Al said he was visiting because he didn't like the senior minister where he was attending.

Karl, however, continued to attend our church.

Over the following months, Karl's emphysema worsened and his doctor visits multiplied. He and his wife had no children, and she was unable to drive, so I called and offered to take him to his treatments. That first trip was a little awkward for both of us, but it was tolerable. The next week he called me and asked if I was available to take him again. I said, "Sure! I'll pick you up half an hour before your appointment." Things were more pleasant that day, and for the next couple of months, I made those bi-weekly trips with Karl, and we became good friends.

On one trip back from the doctor's office, Karl blurted out, "Randy, I voted against you when the elders put you up for minister!"

I had always suspected such, but I was so startled by the admission I didn't respond immediately.

He continued, "But, I think I just wanted them to look at more candidates. Anyway . . . I'm glad you came."

Relieved, I said, "Thanks, Karl. I'm glad I came too."

Not long after that, I was shopping at the local drug store when I "chanced" upon Nick. I spoke first and asked him how he was doing. He told me his doctor visits were increasing in number too. Then Nick said somewhat uncomfortably, "Hey, I appreciate you taking Karl to the doctor. That meant a lot to him."

"I was glad to do it, Nick," I said. Knowing Nick had almost as many doctor visits to make, I added, "If you need that sometime, let me know. We can get better acquainted." Nick thanked me, then we parted ways.

He never took me up on that offer, but nearly a month later, I received a call from his wife, Margaret, telling me he was in the cardiac care unit at Norfolk General Hospital. "He just wanted you to know," she said. To me, that was an invitation to visit him, so I went.

Nick was in a large room with a cluster of wires attached to his chest and tubes to his left arm. Machines surrounding his bed chimed out beats in rhythm with his heart. A couch pushed up to the wall looked like it had been slept in the night before. *Margaret or one of the kids must have spent the night with him*, I thought.

As I walked into the room, Nick and I exchanged courteous greetings, and he asked about the weather outside. "The air's a little chilly this morning," I answered. I wondered if this meeting would be chilly as well.

He said, "It looks nice out the window, but I haven't been out in over a week." Then he looked at me and asked, "What are you doing these days?" I told him some of the news about the church and members he was acquainted with. "You know, Bill's cancer has come back. I just came from visiting him. The good news is, it seems the treatments are taking effect."

"Does he get sick with them?" Nick asked.

"No. He seems to be handling them very well. I'll tell him you asked about him." Nick gave a grateful nod.

I continued, "How about *you*, Nick. How are *you* doing? Do you think you'll be here long?"

He told me his body was rejecting the new heart and unless he had another transplant, his heart would fail. We both knew what that meant: someone would die, probably from an accident, to make another heart available. He struggled with the guilt of someone's death enabling him to live. "It's almost as if I'm anxious for someone to die," he said.

I have since learned this a common feeling among transplant recipients. (In fact, both the recipient and the donor's family struggle with deep-seated emotions.) I also learned later that the hospital put Nick in touch with the family of the donor, and they assured him that his survival gave some meaning to their loved one's sudden death. It helped them to know their loved one's heart was saving Nick's life.

Before I left, the preacher in me had to say, "Nick, I'll pray for the donor's family, and I want the best for you. I'll pray that God give you strength and wisdom through it all. If Margaret needs anything, we'll help her . . ." I paused a moment, then, "Are you ready in case this heart isn't compatible?"

Nick looked down at his hands resting on the sheets, turned them over to look at his palms, then turned them back, palms down again. Taking a deep breath, he said, "I've been thinking about that. I'm ready to go, Randy. I'm just not ready to leave my family." Then he looked at me, waiting for a response.

I looked back into the eyes of a man who deeply loved his family and was concerned about how they would live without him to lead and care for them. "Oh, I understand *that*," I said. Then I prayed with him. From that point on, our relationship was strengthened.

Nick spent the next three months in the hospital hooked up to machines that sustained his heartbeat while he waited for a heart that matched his blood type. The notice had gone to emergency rooms of hospitals across the country. I visited him regularly. He did receive another heart, and his body accepted it. He grew strong and had a good life for another eleven years. He and his family came back to our church, and he became very involved with his Sunday school class. One day I was sitting in my office when I saw Nick carrying a seven-foot table by my door singlehandedly to help set up for a Sunday school class dinner. I thought to myself, *God does work in wondrous ways!*

What I Learned

1. I learned that even Jesus in His humanity had to bear with the weaknesses, imperfections, and failures of His disciples.

2. I learned that we often forget our best experiences with God and easily fall into discouragement.

3. I learned to appreciate spiritual highs when they come but to lean more on the Word of God.

4. I learned that in spite of our weaknesses, God uses us to His glory.

5. I learned to be open to "attitude adjustments."

6. I learned to appreciate the patience of influencers in my life.

7. I learned that to be effective, I must invest my life in others.

8. I learned that I must go beyond what is expected by others.

9. I learned to stay on high ground when faced with conflict.

10. I learned that deep-seated emotions affect outward behaviors and attitudes.

Leadership Application

The purpose of the following is for learning, facilitation of discussion, and preparation for ministry.

1. How would you define a "spiritual high"?

   a. What triggers it?

   b. How long does it last?

   c. Should ministry aim at producing spiritual highs? Why or why not?

   d. Why do people search for spiritual highs, and what are some ways people search for them?

2. In Matthew 17:19–20, Jesus explains that the disciples didn't have enough faith to heal a certain demon-possessed boy.

   a. What are ways you've seen ministry inhibited by lack of faith? How were the results demonstrated?

   b. What are ways we can facilitate a growing faith personally? Corporately?

3. What are the things that frustrate you about ministry and church work?

4. Do some research about people who have left full-time ministry. What reasons are given?

5. How do congregations show their support for ministry?

6. Read Matthew 11:1–5 and Luke 7:18–23. What credentials did Jesus give for his messiahship? Why these?

7. Do you know a church where the members and minister are not on the same page (that is, they seem to have different agendas)?

   a. What are those differences?

   b. What are the results of those differences?

   c. How have those differences been addressed?

8. In what ways are people concerned about their time? Their comfort? Their preferences?

   a. How do each of these concerns affect ministry?

   b. How do you think Jesus would handle these differences?

   c. Can you name instances in the Epistles when Paul dealt with differences? What did he say?

9. Have you ever experienced an attitude adjustment?

   a. What was it, and how did it feel?

   b. What did you learn from it?

10. Have you known a teacher who seemed willing to "pay a price" to be effective? If so, how was that demonstrated?

11. What does "staying on high ground" mean to you?

12. Why does Jesus expect more from us as His followers?

13. What should Kevin have said when Nick thanked him for speaking to his daughter?

14. How would you have handled the conflict between Kevin and Nick?

15. Read Matthew 5:38–48 again. Write a paraphrase, putting it in your own words and in today's setting.

16. Paraphrase Galatians 6:9. How does that scripture influence your ministry?

17. Paraphrase Titus 2:7–8. How does that scripture influence your ministry?

Demonism?

In the darkness of 3 a.m., I could hear her pacing the hall outside my bedroom door. With each pass, she would pause as if listening for movement in my room. I could hear her talking to herself, mumbling something about the devil and demons. Then she would give a low, eerie, muffled laugh. I had played sports in high school and college; I outweighed her by almost sixty pounds, but this woman scared me. *If ever anyone acted like she was demon-possessed*, I thought, *this woman does*.

The woman I'm talking about was my mother's older sister, Madge. For years, she and her husband, John, lived in Gary, West Virginia. They were only fifty miles from our hometown of Grundy, but because of the mountain roads, it took an hour and a half to drive it. John worked as a superintendent in one of the larger coal mines of Gary. He first entered the mine at sixteen and stayed with the same company until he was promoted to a supervisory position. The men he directed were tough and hardened men who, like himself, had grown up in coal territory and worked since they were children. For them, it didn't matter what the weather was like above ground, rain or shine. Deep in the ground it was dark and damp as they worked ten-hour shifts, six days a week.

Of Hungarian descent, John was a big man, brawny and somewhat brutish. He was a man of few words, but he gave you the impression he was competent for any situation. When I was a child, I dreaded their visits because John would pick my dog up by his tail just to watch me squirm. Then, he would laugh boisterously while I pleaded with him to turn my dog loose. Even now, when I hear Jimmy Dean's song "Big Bad John," the image of John Sironko comes to my mind.

Every mornin' at the mine you could see him arrive

He stood six-foot-six and weighed two-forty-five

Kinda broad at the shoulder and narrow at the hip

And everybody knew ya didn't give no lip to big John

He wasn't mean, just . . . well, rough. And not just around the edges, through and through.

Each year, Madge and John would drive to our small town of Grundy, VA to visit with us. I always knew they lived in a different "world" than we and had different values, yet they were polite enough to attend worship with us at the Grundy Church of Christ. Since she had responsibilities at church, mom was grateful for their cooperation. She was also glad they genuinely wanted to attend church with us.

They liked our preacher, Clarence Greenleaf, because he reminded them of their mountainous home in West Virginia. Everyone in Grundy simply called him "Preacher" for as long as I knew him. Though he could be entertaining, interjecting humor in his sermons, he was a hellfire and damnation kind of preacher who shouted and pounded the pulpit. He had a voice that could shake the walls of the room. On one visit after hearing a fiery sermon, Madge volunteered a comment: "Boy! I feel like I've been to church!" His was the kind of preaching they were accustomed to.

Having served the Grundy church for more than thirty-five years, Preacher Greenleaf was more "connected" than any politician in the county. Since he began serving, the attendance had grown from an average of thirty people to a record attendance one Sunday of 1,256. The only person with more connections was the local doctor who had served the town for nearly fifty years!

Preacher Greenleaf's familiarity with people's family history endeared him to many. He had preached the funerals of most parents and grandparents and performed more weddings than any other preacher of the town. He could name siblings, cousins, aunts, and uncles to most of the residents. I once saw him stand up in a restaurant and say, "Now, folks, we oughta thank the Lord. Let's pray." And everyone in the restaurant, believers and nonbelievers alike, out of respect for him, bowed their heads. It was as if they were afraid God would get mad at them if they disrespected the preacher. So no, Madge and John never showed any reluctance at attending church with us, and Mom appreciated it.

By the time I was in college, John had retired and he and Madge moved into a two-bedroom home in Daytona, Florida. Their house was one of those white stucco homes in a clean neighborhood with no black coal dust on the ground. The house didn't have many rooms, but the rooms it did have were spacious. Across the road from their house the Halifax River, part of the Atlantic Intracoastal Waterway, lazily flowed. They often sat in the yard and watched the boats casually sail by their home, occasionally waving at the skipper and crew.

After a few months, John became bored. He didn't know what to do with himself with all the free time retirement afforded, so he started a lawn care business to supplement their income. I remember sitting on his porch with him one afternoon when I asked how he liked retirement. He said simply, "Live like a squirrel. Store food away for the winter."

He and Madge were a fun-loving couple, involved in the party scene wherever they lived. They made friends quickly and enjoyed dressing up on weekends, going to parties, dancing, and drinking alcohol. Alcohol was a constant presence in their home. John would always be seen with a can of beer, and Madge, like a social butterfly at a party, often walked around the house with a highball glass of rum and Coke in one hand and a cigarette in the other, flitting from one part of a room to the other. A constant smile decorated her face.

I remember one afternoon, as they prepared for a dinner party, they both dressed up to the nines and began drinking early. As John patiently waited on Madge to put on her makeup, he stood in her doorway and asked, "Are you right? . . . You right yet?" I assumed that meant, "Are you feeling good? Getting high?" She chuckled and said, "I'm gettin' there."

They had no children of their own and seemed to take an interest in me, sending birthday and Christmas gifts each year. They often invited me to visit them in Daytona. They lived only a couple of miles from Daytona Beach, a famous resort for college students. Spring break afforded me the opportunity to drive there and spend four or five days with them. They were always gracious and welcoming to my visits. However, on my second trip, I noticed significant changes in Madge's personality. She talked about the devil openly to me. At first, I thought this was her attempt at a religious discussion, but what she was saying had no biblical basis and didn't make sense.

One late afternoon I returned to find Madge sitting in the yard, watching the Halifax river flow by. As usual, she had a cigarette in one hand and glass of rum and Coke in the other. I could see she was talking to herself. And for good or bad, I decided to check on her.

"Hi, Madge! Watcha' doin'?"

Madge sat in the lawn chair with one leg crossed over the other and her foot kicking back and forth at a frenetic pace. She reminded me of a two-year-old child forced to sit in a chair and getting restless. She looked up at me, flashed a grin, and said, "Hi, Randy. How was the beach?"

"Great! Better than great! I love it here! There are a lot of kids from different schools visiting the beach."

Madge snickered and pointed to the river. "You see that river? Every night a monster comes out of the water and catches all those kids and eats them up! All those kids in their bathing suits, partying . . ." She snickered again. "He just eats them up, then takes them down to the devil . . ."

Uh oh. I've never heard this before, I thought. I looked around to see if anyone else could have heard her, and I wondered if there was a way I could inconspicuously retreat into the house. I certainly didn't want to upset her. She continued to talk about the devil, demons, and hell. It was as if she were simply giving me information, maybe even sharing gossip and taking pleasure in it. Frankly, she made me nervous. I wouldn't have had anything to do with her except she was my mom's sister and I was a young man from a small town in the mountains who was excited about visiting the beach—Daytona Beach! However, from that point on I became more aware, more sensitive to anything strange, and . . . I became a light sleeper.

More and more I wondered if Madge could somehow be demon-possessed. She seemed fixated on the river and was convinced some "creature" or "monster" was living in it and consuming college students. Throughout the day she would peer out the window or door and stare at the river as if she expected something to come out of it at any minute. She seemed fascinated with the devil and talked about him constantly. Still, nothing moved or levitated on its own, she didn't speak any foreign languages, and her head didn't twist around like an owl's (the way Hollywood depicts it).

I had read there were certain traits and behaviors that could *possibly* characterize demonization. Demons in the New Testament were afraid of Jesus and wanted to avoid Him. Did Madge have an aversion to Christianity? No. She genuinely enjoyed worshiping when with us in Grundy. In the New Testament, demon-possessed people spoke sensibly. Her mind and speech were irrational, but not all the time. A third characteristic was a kind of "supernatural knowledge." Demons in the Bible would know and tell things the possessed person could not know. Madge never displayed anything like that. As far as I could tell, although there were tarot card readers and fortune teller shops along the road leading to her house, she wasn't involved in occult practices—that is, I never saw a Ouija board or tarot cards or any evidence that she had consulted either. Nonetheless, I was very uncomfortable around her.

Nearly fifty years ago, in a series of Bible study tapes for Youth for Christ, author Warren Wiersbe convinced me that the devil is alive and active. He gave four evidences: First, the devil is real, he said, because the *Bible teaches his reality.* Second, the devil is real because *Jesus attested to his reality* and Jesus Christ, who is truth, cannot lie. Third, Wiersbe said, the devil is real because *culture confirms it.* All the evil in our world seems to be a coordinated effort striking against God. Finally, Wiersbe pointed out the devil is real because, if you're honest, *your own experience proves it.* Other writers confirm this fact: The devil "normally works by stirring up temptations in the areas of the seven deadly sins."[1]

A few years after my experience with Madge, I met Ben Alexander, head of E.S.P. (Exposing Satan's Power) Ministries. Ben was a former spiritualist in Britain who converted to Christianity and openly challenged occultists. When attempts were made on his life, he escaped to America and began a ministry exposing the occult. I was enthralled as we sat up past midnight and he told me stories and showed me pictures that made chills run down my spine. Based on the description I gave him, he reassured me that Madge was not possessed by demons. He told me that possession mostly took place in third-world countries, where education was weak and pagan traditions consulted different spirits. "However," he said, "of all the claims by spiritualists in America, 85% are probably false while as many as 15% are genuine."

Madge's conversations and actions were still alarming. But as much as I wondered about her, John seemed to ignore her strange moods and behavior. He obviously felt he didn't need to apologize to anyone for Madge's conversation and behavior. He was very patient with her and simply went on with his daily routine as if nothing was extraordinary.

I made my visits to Daytona for a couple of years and informed my mother after each trip. After getting the report from my second trip, Mom

---

[1] Fr. John Bartunek, LC, "Differences In Demon Possession, Mental Illness, Depression," *SpiritualDirection.com* (blog), November 16, 2017, https://spiritualdirection. com/2017/11/16/differences-in-demon-possession-mental-ilness-or-depression.

was worried enough to call John and talk to him personally about what I had seen and heard.

"John," she began, "this is Alice Childress. How are you?"

John was quick to get rid of the phone. "Alice. Hold on, I'll get Madge."

"No, wait! . . . John? . . . John, I want to talk with *you* first, and I don't want Madge to hear."

John hesitated. "Okay. Go ahead."

This curtness from John was unexpected and made Mom uncomfortable. There was an awkwardness in her voice. "John . . . Randy told me Madge wasn't feeling well while he was there, and I just wanted to check on her. Did he cause any problems while he was there?" I knew Mom was attempting to ease into the issue by suggesting Madge may have been inconvenienced by my visit.

John spoke quickly and deliberately. "No, Alice. Randy was not a problem." He took a breath, then, "Alice, Madge has cancer. There's a tumor on her brain—"

Mom gasped. "Oh, John! What—" This news startled her, and she stammered, "What's going on? What does the doctor say? How bad is it?"

"I think it's terminal."

"What are the doctors telling you?"

"They think the cancer started in her lungs and has spread to her brain. Metas . . . metastasized. We've been getting treatments, but they don't seem to be working."

"Where is she now?" Mom asked.

"She's in bed. She gets headaches, takes pills, and tries to sleep, but she can't sleep. She doesn't eat much either . . . she's lost about twenty pounds since you last saw her. Did Randy tell you?"

"No, he didn't mention that." *Well . . . yeah, now that you mention it, she did look thinner.*

"Oh, John . . . what are we going to do now?"

"We don't know what to do. Just wait on the doctors, I guess. We do everything they tell us to do."

Suddenly, everything began to make sense. A tumor on the front part of her brain was affecting her personality; she wasn't responsible for what she was saying. Trapped within her skull, the growing tumor was pressing against her brain causing severe headaches and blocking vital cerebrospinal fluid that must flow throughout the brain. The alcohol she constantly drank helped dull her headaches. The steroids she took kept her up at night and made her restless. They could also contribute to aggressive behavior. The dimmed lighting in the house, which I thought was an attempt to save electricity, was an effort to ease her headaches. The tumor and chemotherapy were causing hallucinations; she was seeing things that weren't there. It turned out Madge was a sweet, considerate woman who wanted to spare people her troubles. She didn't want to burden anyone. John, in his love for her, would do what he needed to do to protect her both physically and emotionally. My whole perspective changed.

Over the next few months Mom called John weekly to check on Madge. He gradually became more open and obliging with the latest updates. He kept Mom up to date on Madge's medicine, chemotherapy, and radiation treatments . . . and that they seemed to make no progress. Surgery had been ruled out; the prognosis wasn't good. That was when Mom decided to take action. Of all people she called her preacher!

Preacher Greenleaf had the same way of answering the telephone every time. He intended to say, "Yeah, hello," but it always came out, "Yel-lo." He had an upbeat tempo to this voice whenever talking on the phone—one that communicated, *I'm glad you called.*

"Preacher, this is Alice."

"Well hellooo, honey darlin'! How *are* you?"

"Preacher, you remember my sister Madge and her husband John from Daytona. I just found out Madge has cancer, and it doesn't look good for her."

Preacher Greenleaf had heard this kind of news many times in nearly forty years as the minister of a large church. He not only heard from members of the Grundy congregation, but also from non-members who called because he had preached a parent's funeral or conducted their friend's wedding. As many times as he had received these kinds of calls, he had never hardened himself to them but remained kindhearted.

"Oh, Alice. I'm so sorry. I like them both. What's going on with her?"

Mom went on to describe the kind and severity of Madge's cancer as well as the treatments that had been ineffective.

"But, Preacher, the reason I'm calling is that Madge is not a Christian. Neither she nor John have ever made that decision. They love you and respect you, and I thought I would ask . . . would you be willing to go to Daytona and talk with them . . . while she has time? Ralph and I will pay your expenses, and Randy will go with you."

"Why YES! Of course I'll go."

Preacher Greenleaf was not a procrastinator, and he took seriously the mission he had just been handed—a mission he believed from the Lord God Himself! We made plans to leave at 2 a.m. the next morning.

Seven-hundred-plus miles had us driving nearly eleven hours, stopping only to grab fast food and use the bathroom. The whole trip I wondered,

How can I prepare him for Madge's unpredictable behavior? With about 100 miles to go, I thought, *If I'm going to do it, I better do it now.* Preacher was driving as I began the conversation.

"Preacher?"

"Yes?"

"I think I need to warn you about Madge. This tumor has affected her mind, and she says things that are really off the wall. In fact, I'm thinking she may even be hostile."

"Oh?" He never took his eyes off the road.

"Yes, she talks about the devil a lot, and for a long time I thought she might be possessed! Well . . . what I'm saying is, she may not be very receptive to us or what we're going to tell her."

Without turning his eyes from the road, he reached his right hand over and patted my knee. "Okay. I gotcha. If this is what the Lord wants, the devil won't get in the way. The Lord will see to it. Jehovah-Jireh."

He doesn't know what he's in for, I thought.

When we crossed the Volusia County line, Preacher Greenleaf said we would stop first at a Daytona church he was familiar with and ask to use their baptistery. *We haven't even talked to Madge yet,* I thought, *and he's already making plans to baptize her! Gonna be embarrassing if we get kicked out of their house and have to explain to this minister we drove all this way to baptize someone who didn't want to be baptized.*

As soon as we walked into the Holly Hill Church of Christ building, the residing minister, Chuck Estep, immediately recognized Preacher Greenleaf from previous conventions and revivals. After exchanging greetings, Preacher filled him in on our purpose and asked if we could use the baptistry. The minister gave his approval and promised to have everything ready. Then another conversation developed.

Preacher Greenleaf had asked Chuck how things were going for him. Now, his welcoming, jubilant mood became sober as he told us challenges ministry had in Daytona Beach.

"Greenleaf, this area is known as the 'psychic headquarters of the world!' San Francisco may be the spiritualist headquarters, but less than a half hour drive from here is a place called Cassadaga that has more spiritists per capita than any other."

He went on to tell us of the number of mediums, fortune tellers, and spiritualists in his area. Both Preacher Greenleaf and I sat on the edge of our seats. Cassadaga had been established nearly a century earlier by a self-professed medium, who claimed to communicate with the dead.

"This is now a place where celebrities, politicians, and the rich come for fortune-telling and séances. They're desperate people looking for guidance in all the wrong places!"

Preacher just shook his head. "My, my, my! Lord have mercy!"

Time was passing quickly, and Preacher Greenleaf decided we needed to go. He led us in prayer, Chuck continued in prayer, and I closed.

It was about 4 p.m. when we pulled into John and Madge's driveway. I reached for my door handle, but Preacher took hold of my arm. "Wait, Randy! We need to pray before we go in." I sat back in the seat while Preacher prayed, and I wondered what John would think if he noticed two men in a strange car sitting in his driveway with their heads bowed.

This wasn't a short prayer like Peter's "Lord, help me!" as he was sinking. This was a long, pronounced prayer with praise and thanksgiving for a safe trip and for opportunity to share the gospel. Preacher was animated as he prayed. I could feel the car rocking side to side as he shifted in his seat and moved his arms in expression. Finally, Preacher came to the point, Madge and John.

Though my eyes were closed, I could hear him thumping the steering wheel with the heels of his hands. He wasn't just saying words in this prayer; he was fighting a battle, genuinely engaging in conflict and seeking resources from his Commander in Chief.

Immediately I thought of Elijah on Mt. Carmel, openly declaring the glory of God in the presence of the enemy. He challenged the devil, almost taunting him to face Almighty God. This unnerved me at first, until I remembered that after the confrontation on the Mount of Temptation, Satan and his demons tried to avoid Jesus at all costs.

In his prayer, Preacher Greenleaf claimed the work of the cross. Then he professed the name of Jesus, recalling Peter's preaching of forgiveness and mercy and healing. From memory, he quoted Philippians 2:9-11: "Therefore God exalted him to the highest place and gave him the name that is above every name, that at the name of Jesus every knee should bow, in heaven and on earth and under the earth, and every tongue acknowledge that Jesus Christ is Lord, to the glory of God the Father."

Three steps led up to the door, and I rang the doorbell from the second step. When John opened it he stood in the doorway and stared at us for a moment. I had forgotten how intimidating his stature was. Even at sixty-six, he was physically fit, and standing there he looked to me as if he were ten feet tall.

"Hi, John," I said. "Mom called and told you we were coming. Remember Preacher Greenleaf?"

John looked at Preacher and nodded. "Yeah. C'mon in." He stepped back, opening the door wide enough for us to enter and then closing it behind us.

Preacher stepped up beside John, put his arm around John's shoulder, and spoke with all the compassion and understanding he could muster. "John, oh, John!" That was all he had to say. Just those simple words and the tone of his voice communicated Preacher's love for them.

John dropped his head and stifled a sob.

Preacher had been in situations like this countless times before, standing next to a spouse who had just lost her husband; next to a parent who's child had died in an accident. He knew their suffering and just his presence and tone of his voice gave them solace.

"Bless your heart, John . . . this has been so hard for you, I know." John couldn't hold it back anymore. He bowed his head and cried. This hulk of a man, John Sironko, probably hadn't cried since he was an infant. He was no longer tough. Now he was broken. He had used up all his resources, financially, physically and emotionally, for the woman he loved. He had come to the end of himself.

Preacher swung around front of John and now put both arms around John's shoulders, pulling him in. The two men stood there for a few moments, embracing each other. It impressed me then as it does now. I was seeing God reach down from heaven and comfort John through Preacher Greenleaf.

"Tell us how things are," Preacher said.

We moved into the dimly lit living room. Preacher pulled his chair over next to John, and put his hand on John's shoulder. "What are the doctors saying now?"

Doctors had given Madge weeks, or at best maybe a couple of months. We listened as he described the medicines and reactions and disappointments they both had experienced. With no children or immediate family in the area, John had taken care of her the best he knew how. He was alone and helpless, unfamiliar territory for him.

Preacher spoke up. "Is she conscious? Is she aware?"

"Yes," John replied.

"Can we see her now?"

John didn't answer. He just stood and pointed to Madge's bedroom door.

The room was dimly lit by a window off to my right. Curtains were half-closed, and behind them sheers filtered any light coming into the room. On the opposite side of the room, a large king-size bed was positioned in the middle of the wall. Tall lamps were on each side of the bed, but they were turned off. Above the headboard was a large portrait of John and Madge, in their early forties. Flanking each side of the portrait were framed photos of their wedding.

Lying prone on the bed, Madge's head was heavily bandaged from biopsies and treatments. She didn't move, and at first I thought she was asleep. *Maybe we shouldn't disturb her right now. She's resting.*

John walked over and gently rubbed two fingers up and down Madge's arm, calling her by name. "Madge, wake up! You've got company. Wake up." Then he walked over, leaned back on the register below the window, and crossed his arms.

Madge began to stir, and I tensed up. *What if her condition's deteriorated and she's become violent? What if in an outburst she throws things at Preacher? What if she throws a profanity-laced tirade at Preacher?* I looked at John and saw he was relaxed, so I figured there was nothing to worry about.

Preacher Greenleaf took hold of a chair in the room, dragged it over next to the bed, and sat there. Then he reached down and took Madge's hand. "Madge? Madge darlin', do you know who I am?"

Madge slowly turned her head toward him, looked at him for a moment, and feebly said, "Why, yes . . . you're Preacher Greenleaf, and you've come to talk to me about Jesus."

What?! That's it?! No talk about the devil, demons, or monsters in the river? I looked over to John, who was standing now, mouth open and arms to his side. I looked at Preacher, who showed no surprise at all. And I looked at Madge. Her eyes were welling up with tears.

"Yes, darlin', I'm going to talk to you about Jesus."

Preacher opened his Bible and laid it on the bed next to Madge. For the next fifteen minutes he presented the gospel while John, now standing by the headboard, listened to every word. Preacher told them he wanted to baptize them and had made arrangements at the Holly Hills Church of Christ just down the road from their house. They agreed, and Preacher and I went in the living room and waited till John got Madge ready. A few minutes later, the bedroom door opened and John came out pushing Madge in a wheelchair. She smiled at us and said, her voice still weak, "I'm ready!"

John drove us all in his car since it was bigger and had a rack on the back for Madge's wheelchair. Preacher spoke up. "John, you know, you need to do this too."

"I gonna do it!" John said.

We placed Madge in a folding chair from the church. I took hold of the chair's front legs, while John held tightly on its back. As I picked up the front legs, John lowered Madge into a reclining position. Together we carried her into the baptistry where Preacher was waiting. The water had been warmed, and preacher asked Madge if she was comfortable. She said she was, so he continued.

"Madge, if you believe in Jesus repeat after me: I, Madge Sironko . . ."

"I, Madge Sironko . . ."

". . . believe Jesus is the Christ, the Son of the living God."

". . . believe Jesus . . . the Son of the living God."

"And I take Him as my Lord and my Savior."

". . . I take Him as my Lord and Savior."

Preacher lifted his head upward, raised his left hand high with his right hand on Madge's forehead, and said, "By the power and authority of our Lord and Savior, Jesus Christ, I baptize you, Madge Sironko, for the remission of every sin you have committed, in the name of the Father, the Son, and the Holy Ghost." Then he nodded at John, and John lowered Madge back into the water, only for a second, and raised her immediately. Madge started sobbing, reached back, and put her hand on John's hand that was resting on her shoulder. John started crying. I started crying. The host preacher was crying and clapping. Preacher was just smiling. "Praise the Lord! Praise the Lord! O Praise God!" he said.

John and I lifted the chair and carried Madge up out of the baptistry, then John turned walked back down and stood next to Preacher. Preacher asked him to confess his faith in Jesus. He did. On his own he leaned back, and Preacher caught him, then lowered him into the water and lifted him up again. Madge sat at the top landing, hands clasped, smiling.

On the way back to the house there was laughter and conversation. After about another half hour, Preacher Greenleaf and I left for an eleven-hour return home.

Mom held tissue to her mouth while we told her about Madge and John's decision. She wept joyfully, reached out, and hugged Preacher, then me. Dad reached over and took Preacher's hand in his and thanked him repeatedly, then put his arm around my shoulders and hugged me.

That night, Mom began a series of phone calls to her two brothers and other three sisters to give them the news of Madge's baptism. She and the sisters orchestrated a family reunion. Three weeks later, all of Madge's siblings with their families drove to Daytona to visit and see her. For the two days we were there, Madge was able to sit up in the wheelchair, her head covered with a bandana, and carry on intelligent conversation with everyone. Even though Madge had received a terminal prognosis, everyone wanted these few hours to be filled with love and joy. There was no irrational talk but pleasant conversations, as God had given Madge a clear mind. There was no somberness, but there was laughter at their reminiscences of childhood.

A little over a month later, John called Mom to tell her Madge had passed. "It was peaceful," he said. "She wasn't in pain." Mom said John was at peace too.

What I Learned

- I learned to appreciate older, wiser, and more experienced preachers.

- I learned the real battle in ministry is conducted through prayer.

- I learned to differentiate between physical, emotional, and spiritual issues.

- I learned to ask, "Have you had a physical examination lately?"

- I learned NOTHING is impossible to God.

- I learned to rejoice at EVERY conversion, even at the deathbed.

Leadership Application

1. Who are the ministers most respected in your community and why?

2. In your view, what examples by ministers are the most important and why?

3. Would it have been better for my mother to call the preacher residing in Daytona rather than sending Preacher Greenleaf? Why or why not?

4. Review the book of Acts and make a list of occasions when prayer was employed by the apostles and the early church. How was prayer employed in each?

5. Review the Gospels. What characteristics of demon possession were the most obvious?

6. Differentiate between those and the portrayals of demons in TV shows, movies, and other media.

7. What does the Bible say about occult practices? (King Saul consulted a witch.)

8. Read Deuteronomy 29:29. What currently common practices violate this command?

9. What do clients of fortune tellers and mediums hope to gain?

10. Read the following scriptures and paraphrase them in your own words, applying them to ministry:

a. 1 Samuel 17:47

b. Ephesians 6:10–20

c. Philippians 4:6–7

d. 1 Peter 5:8–9

11. In what ways can people mistake a tumor, a mood disorder, or depression for demonic activity?

12. Conduct a private survey among ten anonymous friends to learn how they feel about deathbed conversions.

13. Read and paraphrase in your own words:

a. Hebrews 3:7–8, 14

b. Hebrews 4:7

c. 2 Corinthians 6:2

14. What concerns are raised with deathbed conversions and how would you address those concerns?

15. Read Matthew 20:1–16 and tell this story in a contemporary application.

Beware the Media

Carolyn Garrett was an elementary school principal held in high esteem by school staff and parents alike. She was also highly respected among school administrators and was not without influence in a larger public arena, serving as an adjunct professor at a college and as an Arts Commissioner for the City of Virginia Beach. Upon first meeting her, you would be impressed as much with her professional bearing as her personality. A tall, slender, engaging woman, she had a Southern charm that made her immediately likeable. It was to our benefit that Carolyn was also a devoted member of Kempsville Church.

Carolyn grew up in a strong Christian home in the Piedmont region of North Carolina. Both her mother and father loved the Lord and served Him faithfully within their country church. Her parents' love for the Lord and His church passed on to her. From playing on the women's softball team to singing in the choir to serving on dozens of committees and supporting her husband (who was an elder), she was integral to the church fellowship.

Carolyn loves children and saw public education as her niche. As a public school teacher and principal, she influenced thousands of children in her tenure through a multitude of creative programs. Among the projects that interested me in particular was a character development program she co-authored called the Character Approach to Problem Solving. When she described this campaign to me, I immediately recognized many of the biblical traits called the fruit of the Spirit:

But the fruit of the Spirit is love, joy, peace, forbearance,
kindness, goodness, faithfulness, gentleness and self-control.
Against such things there is no law. (Galatians 5:22–23)

I wondered, was there a way we could join hands to promote synonymous qualities? Then I had a light bulb moment. Why not hold a special event called Churches and Schools Working Together to Build Character in the Community? This, I thought, might be a great way to influence our community and get interested families to the church.

I followed through with this idea and along with Carolyn recruited Dr. Marshall Leggett, former president of Milligan College (a Christian liberal arts college) as well as Dr. George Harvey, a licensed professional counselor to whom I had referred families for more than ten years. This was going to be a great program!

Putting everything into place I could think of, I launched into an advertising campaign and contacted the media, hoping for free publicity through local news sources. You know, headlines like, "GOOD things happening in your community!" I printed posters and handouts, made phone calls, and wrote dozens of letters.

Then it happened.

A reporter from the local newspaper wanted to interview both Carolyn and me by telephone for more information. *This is great!* I thought. *The local newspaper will publish and help us advertise our program.* I contacted Carolyn to learn the most convenient time for her and then notified the reporter.

On the day of the phone interview, Carolyn joined me at the church office. Right on time, the reporter called. He began the interview by asking me questions about my ministry at Kempsville: How long have you been at this church? How many people attend this church? What is your purpose in presenting the program? Who are the speakers? Why are they relevant to the program? The conversation we had was cordial, and I was already anticipating a positive news report.

After these questions, he asked to speak to Mrs. Garrett. Carolyn gave a cheerful "Hello! How are you?" I couldn't hear his voice, but he apparently told her that he was familiar with her popularity as a public school principal. Carolyn graciously thanked him for the compliments and asked him how his day was going. The next words I heard from Carolyn were, "No . . . no . . . no . . . you're confused about the nature of this program. No, that's not what's happening here, and if you print that, I will take you to task." She was firm but pleasantly composed in her responses to his questions.

After a few more questions and answers, Carolyn prodded me to take the handset saying, "He'd like to speak to you now." It must have been apparent that I was puzzled by what I had just heard, because she smiled and prodded me to take the handset.

"Hello, this is Randy," I said puzzled by the one-sided conversation I'd heard . There was a long pause, then I could hear him take a deep breath on the other end of the phone and say, "It *still* makes me nervous to talk to a principal!" I smiled at that and looked at Carolyn, who was sitting opposite me, still smiling and unruffled by the interview. I could tell she had dealt with reporters before, and I thought, *That's a talent I wish I had.*

After the call, I was disappointed to learn he had questioned her involvement in the program and insinuated she may be violating the "separation of church and state" by participating in a religious setting as a public school leader. I suppose I was naïve, but I was dumbfounded to think anyone might not be happy that schools and churches could agree on the need to strengthen character in children. I understood that schools and churches had different approaches to these goals but had hoped we could at least unite to put a spotlight on solutions. After all, I had done this before by participating in a 1995 panel discussion WHRO-TV, the local public broadcasting station.

The Tidewater Mediation Center had assembled four panelists, two who were opposed to abortion and two in favor of making abortion more available. On one side, a preacher (me), and on the other side favoring abortion on demand was the current director of the local Planned Parenthood Center. The subject of the discussion was "Abortion: Seeking Common Ground in Hampton Roads." It was aired immediately after a documentary featuring the story of a twenty-seven-year-old mother of two who had died after a botched abortion performed by her lover in a motel room.

Why on earth would a pro-life adherent participate in such a panel? Especially after *that* horrible film? My thinking was, we could perhaps agree on fewer unplanned pregnancies *resulting* in fewer abortions. Of course, I was advocating abstinence, keeping sex within the confines of a traditional marriage.

Here's what Larry Bonko, columnist for the Virginian Pilot, wrote the next day: "After this 'P.O.V.' film, it takes courage to go on camera and take a stand against legal, presumably safe abortion. Childress did that with grace while making an important point: 'If all the energy, enthusiasm and resources involved on both sides could be put into a single direction, imagine what could be accomplished.'"[1] (Thus, I do not believe ministers should shy away from public discourse on moral issues.) Reading his review of my participation encouraged me.

The church and school program went on as planned. There was a warmness about the evening as Carolyn expressed best interests in the welfare of children, Dr. Leggett described the changes that were taking place in many colleges across the nation, and family counselor Dr. Harvey explained the need for moral anchors in children. Nearly 200 people from the community attended and expressed gratitude. I breathed a sigh of relief the next morning that there were no negative editorials, articles, or abusive letters aimed at us in the newspaper.

This experience, however, added to my growing wariness of the news media. I've come to the conclusion that the **news media thrives on controversy**. On March 15, 2018, a bridge in Florida collapsed,

---

[1] Larry Bonko, "Documentary Focuses Debate On Abortion," *The Virginian-Pilot*, November 28, 1995, p. E2.

tragically killing several people. As would be expected, this was an event that generated concern about the nation's road and transportation infrastructure. Architects, engineers, and contractors as well as the Department of Transportation and Safety investigated to determine causes of the collapse. For weeks, news outlets across the country published reports. One engineer I know was contacted by a local reporter the day after the collapse to ask what might have gone wrong.

When he told me about the upcoming interview, I responded, "Be careful." "Why?" he asked. I cautioned him by posing a possible headline: "Local Engineer Blames Bridge Collapse on Faulty Design and Construction." He responded, "No, that would not be good." He chose not to give the interview.

At times the news media can appear to be "ravenous wolves," seizing on tragedy and crisis; however, they rightly see themselves as protectors of our freedoms. They see themselves as crusaders to right perceived wrongs, as communicators to guide the uninformed.

The American Press Institute states this on its website: "The purpose of journalism is thus to provide citizens with the information they need to make the best possible decisions about their lives, their communities, their societies, and their governments."[2]

Not all reporters are assailants of Christianity. Not all reporters have insidious motives. However, the temptation toward sensationalism seems to be inherent within the secular media. Headlines are highlighted in bold print and worded in ways that are designed to draw attention. Even broadcast news media begins national news programs with dramatic music designed to catch attention. Announcers use urgent tones in their voices as they describe the topics to come in the next thirty minutes. (It is true that people often ignore warnings, as in the case of approaching hurricanes, so

---

[2] "What is the purpose of journalism?" *American Press Institute*, accessed May 1, 2019, https://www.americanpressinstitute.org/journalism-essentials/what-is-journalism/purpose-journalism/.

urgency is sometimes justified.) These methods can highlight, intensify, or even create dynamic controversy.

WHAT CAN WE DO?

Through many experiences in dealing with the media, both good and bad, I've learned some valuable lessons. They are the following:

Stay current and relevant

Ministers are often accused of naiveté, living in an ivory tower, protected from the problems and issues their congregants experience. When church members feel that way, they are more likely to separate their faith from everyday living and ignore the preacher's counsel.

As always, people are living under intense pressure. Single parents dealing with teenage angst; divorcees finding themselves with reduced income; salesmen pressured to lie or offer inappropriate incentives to make a sale; employees suffering threats and abuse from their supervisors; women who were molested when they were children, never able to forget, never able to forgive. People typically think church leaders are disconnected from real life . . . *their* lives. We would be wrong to give them that impression

Theologian Karl Barth is generally credited with saying that every preacher "should have a Bible in one hand and a newspaper in the other." Another quote attributed to him is, "Take your Bible and take your newspaper, and read both. But interpret newspapers from your Bible."[1]

Barth's emphasis is well taken. We must be aware of current events and be relevant, *and* we must be discerning. Jesus warned his disciples, "I am sending you out like sheep among wolves. Therefore be as shrewd as snakes and as innocent as doves" (Matthew 10:16).

---

[1] "Frequently Asked Questions" *Princeton Theological Seminary*, accessed May 1, 2019, http://barth.ptsem.edu/about-cbs/faq.

1 Chronicles 12:32 describes the men who joined exiled David in Hebron as "men who understood the times and knew what Israel should do." We must be people who "understand the times" to effectively communicate the gospel and conduct ministry.

On the topic of discernment, the Bible also has this to say:

> See to it that no one takes you captive through hollow and deceptive philosophy, which depends on human tradition and the elemental spiritual forces of this world rather than on Christ. (Colossians 2:8)

> But solid food is for the mature, who by constant use have trained themselves to distinguish good from evil. (Hebrews 5:14)

> Dear friends, do not believe every spirit, but test the spirits to see whether they are from God, because many false prophets have gone out into the world. (1 John 4:1)

Understand the biases of media resources

A 2005 posting on the Student News Daily website attempts to define the differences between conservatives and liberals.[2] The article lists twenty-one issues such as abortion, education, embryonic stem cell research, euthanasia and physician-assisted suicide, gun control, global warming, immigration, and same-sex marriage. These are many of the issues that divide the country. Your view on these issues will determine whether you are politically liberal, conservative, or somewhere between. Whatever the issue, our views must be governed by the Word of God: "We demolish arguments and every pretension that sets itself up against the knowledge of God, and we take captive every thought to make it obedient to Christ" (2 Corinthians 10:5).

---

[2] "Conservative vs. Liberal Beliefs," *StudentNewsDaily.com*, 2010, https://www.studentnewsdaily.com/conservative-vs-liberal-beliefs/.

The secular media, however, has no biblical imperatives or restraints. A 2004 Pew Research Center article states, "Fully 91% of those who work at national news organizations say it is not necessary to believe in God to be moral."[3]

BEWARE = be aware

Choose your resources carefully. After more than fifty years of reading local newspapers, I cancelled my subscription to the newspaper servicing our city. For the next month I received weekly calls from the newspaper office asking me to re-subscribe and then finally asking my reason for cancelling. I gave them two: (1) The articles had become *too explicit*. I explained that the article that had sent me over the edge told of a man who had pimped his wife and described what the husband required of her. I felt this was too much information and was totally unnecessary. (2) The *slant* of articles and editorials had become *too steep* for me. I felt I could no longer subsidize opinions and reporting I considered to be contrary to Scripture.

Before that, I had begun to notice a growing focus in much of the news media toward hypocrisy in politics, business, and especially the church. When hypocrisy is exposed among religious institutions, God is held in reproach by unbelievers. That is not the media's fault; we must not give them ammunition to use against us. There must not be even the suggestion of wrongdoing, because integrity is essential to Christian witness: "But among you there must not be even a hint of sexual immorality, or of any kind of impurity, or of greed, because these are improper or God's holy people" (Ephesians 5:3). The media has a right to expect honesty in our speech and behavior. (See 1 Peter 1:13, 5:8; Ephesians 6:18.)

Maintain balance

We are bombarded from every side with messages. How do we maintain proper balance? Every thought, word, and action must be evaluated by its

---

[3] "Bottom-Line Pressures Now Hurting Coverage, Say Journalists," *Pew Research Center*, May 23, 2004, https://www.people-press.org/2004/05/23/iv-values-and-the-press/.

effect on the name of Christ. That evaluation would be based on the Word of God.

Matthew 6:33 – "But seek first his kingdom and his righteousness, and all these things will be given to you as well."

2 Peter 3:17 – "Therefore, dear friends, since you have been forewarned, be on your guard so that you may not be carried away by the error of the lawless and fall from your secure position."

Philippians 4:8–9 – "Finally, brothers and sisters, whatever is true, whatever is noble, whatever is right, whatever is pure, whatever is lovely, whatever is admirable—if anything is excellent or praiseworthy—think about such things. Whatever you have learned or received or heard from me, or seen in me—put it into practice. And the God of peace will be with you."

Hebrews 5:14 – "But solid food is for the mature, who by constant use have trained themselves to distinguish good from evil."

Proverbs 15:21 – "whoever has understanding keeps a straight course."

Proverbs 18:15 – "The heart of the discerning acquires knowledge, for the ears of the wise seek it out."

Romans 12:2 – "Do not conform to the pattern of this world, but be transformed by the renewing of your mind. Then you will be able to test and approve what God's will is—his good, pleasing and perfect will."

Acts 17:11 – "Now the Berean Jews were of more noble character than those in Thessalonica, for they received the message with great eagerness and examined the Scriptures every day to see if what Paul said was true."

Refuse to feed the controversies

The Bible puts parameters around our conversations:

1 Timothy 6:3–5 – "These are the things you are to teach and insist on. If anyone teaches otherwise and does not agree to the sound instruction of our Lord Jesus Christ and to godly teaching, they are conceited and understand nothing. They have an unhealthy interest in controversies and quarrels about words that result in envy, strife, malicious talk, evil suspicions and constant friction between people of corrupt mind, who have been robbed of the truth and who think that godliness is a means to financial gain."

Titus 3:9–11 – "But avoid foolish controversies and genealogies and arguments and quarrels about the law, because these are unprofitable and useless. Warn a divisive person once, and then warn them a second time. After that, have nothing to do with them. You may be sure that such people are warped and sinful; they are self-condemned."

That is, don't be contentious, always looking for a fight. Answer issues biblically, spiritually, and graciously. Don't be argumentative, combative, or condescending. Constant quarrelling is ineffective and counterproductive. Bob Russell, retired minister at Southeast Christian Church in Louisville, said, "The adversary today portrays anybody who stands for biblical values as ignorant, intolerant, part of a fringe minority."[4]

2 Timothy 2:14–15 – " Keep reminding God's people of these things. Warn them before God against quarreling about words; it is of no value, and only ruins those who listen. Do your best to present yourself to God

---

[4] Bob Russell, "Making the Most of Our Opportunities,"

as one approved, a worker who does not need to be ashamed and who correctly handles the word of truth."

*****

EMPLOYING (USING) THE MEDIA

Dangers of using the media

There are a number of problems associated with using the media. Here are a few:

- **Most media is biased.** As already shown, the mass media generally leans to the liberal side, and I don't just mean politically. When I began ministry forty-five years ago, I never dreamed abortion and same-sex marriage could become legal in America, a heretofore "Christian" nation. I'm amazed how rapidly they have occurred. Certainly the media hastened their acceptance through news reports, movies, TV, and music. As I write, congress is debating the legalization of letting an infant die after birth.[5]

- **Most media is not interested in church matters.** In fact, larger media groups give very little credence to church work. We rarely hear of the good work churches are doing because people expect the church to be involved in good works. It's "newsworthy" when businesses or clubs do them, embellishing secular humanism. Smaller communities, however, are more open to community faith news.

- **Letters to the editor may draw negative responses.** In fact, you can count on it. While you can expect to see negative responses to

---

[5] Mike DeBonis and Felicia Sonmez, "Senate blocks bill on medical care for children born alive after attempted abortion," *The Washington Post*, February 25, 2019, https://www.washingtonpost.com/politics/senate-blocks-bill-on-medical-care-for-children-born-alive-after-attempted-abortion/2019/02/25/e5d3d4d8-3924-11e9-a06c-3ec8ed509d15_story.html?utm_term=.b4e2fec17c04.

your letter to the editor, you rarely get the opportunity to rebut or correct their misconceptions. Most newspapers limit consecutive letters from the same author.

- **Letters to the editor may draw activists.** This is a very real possibility. After my article supporting traditional marriage between one man and one woman, there were not only negative responses for the next few days, but the following Sunday we had three surprise visitors at our morning worship service. Shortly after I began preaching, these three young men walked down the aisle in view of the entire congregation while wearing dresses. If they expected an angry response, they did not get one. Other than being polite and welcoming, we did not give them any attention but continued to worship. When it became obvious we weren't going to confront them, they made a show of themselves storming out just before I said the closing prayer.

    We had expected something like this and were prepared for it. We resolved we would treat the activists with the same courtesy we showed to all visitors—our services were open to everyone—but would not give activists the negative attention they wanted. We also determined beforehand we would not tolerate public displays of affection on church property from either homo or hetero couples.
- **Media's right to edit.** Another problem with writing articles or letters to the editor is their right to edit for space. Editing can reword the title, the content, and the tone of your message, sometimes making your message harsher than intended.

Tips for submitting letters or articles to the media

Many non-churched people have negative perceptions about churches. You have opportunities to present good, effective witness to them through various media outlets. The following suggestions may help.

- **Don't sound angry. Be gracious.** Colossians 4:5–6 – "Conduct yourselves with wisdom toward outsiders, making the most of the opportunity. Let your speech always be with grace, as though seasoned with salt, so that you will know how you should respond to each person."

Most non-churched people know what we're against but not what we're for. Be sure to provide balance. For example, if writing about homosexuality, be sure to provide the benefits of the biblical viewpoint.

- **Parse your words**. When writing letters to the editor, scrutinize your content and intent carefully. Is there anything in your submission that can be misinterpreted?

Think of it, almost every city has a media and communications manager who releases information to the public, as do businesses and sports teams. The president has a press secretary whose job is to make the president look good to the media. Political leaders understand the press corps will often dig to find fault. We must take care how and what we say since our presentation is a reflection on Christ.

- **Be savvy**. As powerful as the news media is, it is a highly competitive field. They compete with other forms of media. I realized this when the *Virginian Pilot* published my lengthy letter to the editor as an article on the opinion page. My submission expressed concern that television programming was contributing to the escalating rate of violence.

- **Be brief**. The average newspaper allows approximately 800 words for an article and less than 300 words for a letter to the editor. If more, the tone your article or letter may be substantially altered.

- **Anticipate objections**. Write in such a way as to reduce negative responses. Newspapers love ongoing controversy (as long as they control it). A lawyer or debater will always take time to anticipate how their own reasons and arguments can be turned against them. Anticipate the objections and answer them before they are raised.

I don't mean to dissuade use of the media, but I am suggesting that we be mindful of how our programs and promotions can be interpreted.

Proverbs 14:8 says, "The wisdom of the prudent is to give thought to their ways." Colossians 4:5 reaffirms that admonition: "Be wise in the way you act toward outsiders; make the most of every opportunity." The mistake I made with the church and school program was in not considering how secular minds would perceive our character program. I should have anticipated and addressed their concerns at the beginning.

Raise Up Christian journalists

There's no doubt in my mind that the media influences culture. If not responsible for the culture we see today, the media has certainly hastened the changes, whether for good or bad.

News Media Alliance reports that 96% of television viewers still watch news on a TV set, 88% listen to the radio offline, and 79% still read a printed newspaper.[6]

Since the media is as influential as it is, we must send Christian young people into this market to influence it for Christ. This means young people must be taught biblical truth in churches regarding the controversial issues rampant in our society. Certainly social issues should not absorb the entire youth program, but they should be given proportionate attention. Perhaps a college prep class for high school seniors could help prepare students for the pressures they will experience in college. Secular colleges challenge young believers to question everything they believe about God. Because of my education in biology, one public school teacher suggested I visit the city school administration building to discover when evolution would be taught and teach the creation view to our youth. Not wanting young people to receive it as a "battle cry" and go into the classroom armed for conflict against an older, more experienced authority, I chose rather to teach creation at other times of the year (usually summer months).

---

[6] Rebecca Frank, "New Data Show News Media Is Stronger Than Ever," *News Media Alliance*, June 1, 2018, https://www.newsmediaalliance.org/data-news-media-stronger/.

Many parents are uncomfortable with their church talking to their children about sensitive topics, but the schools, media, and their peers do not hesitate to shape the morality of our youth. Christian parents and churches must cooperate to present a united stance on the faith.

> Dear friends, although I was very eager to write to you about the salvation we share, I felt compelled to write and urge you to **contend for the faith** that was once for all entrusted to God's holy people . . .
>
> But, dear friends, remember what the apostles of our Lord Jesus Christ foretold. They said to you, "In the last times there will be scoffers who will follow their own ungodly desires." These are the people who divide you, who follow mere natural instincts and do not have the Spirit.
>
> But you, dear friends, by building yourselves up in your most holy faith and praying in the Holy Spirit, keep yourselves in God's love as you wait for the mercy of our Lord Jesus Christ to bring you to eternal life.
>
> Be merciful to those who doubt; save others by snatching them from the fire; to others show mercy, mixed with fear—hating even the clothing stained by corrupted flesh.
>
> To him who is able to keep you from stumbling and to present you before his glorious presence without fault and with great joy—to the only God our Savior be glory, majesty, power and authority, through Jesus Christ our Lord, before all ages, now and forevermore! Amen. (Jude 1:3, 17–25)

I'm glad to say there is a growing contingent of Christian news people. An online search reveals a number of colleges and universities offering Christian journalism programs. May their tribe increase!

Make your community aware of the church's contributions

Some church members don't want attention drawn to their works, citing Matthew 6:3: "But when you give to the needy, do not let your left hand know what your right hand is doing." However, Jesus also said, "let your light shine before others, *that they may see your good deeds and glorify your Father in heaven*" (Matthew 5:16, author's emphasis).

I appreciate people who refuse to receive glory for themselves, but Jesus said we should let people see our works and give them opportunity to glorify God. In fact, the very purpose of our good works is to draw attention to God. If all your community knows about the church is what they see in unflattering news reports, the community is being deprived of a powerful witness.

Jesus didn't hide His works. He went throughout Galilee teaching in their synagogues, proclaiming the good news of the kingdom, and healing every disease and sickness among the people. News about Him spread all over Syria, and people brought to Him all who were ill with various diseases, those suffering severe pain, the demon-possessed, those with epilepsy, and the paralyzed, and He healed them (Matthew 4:23–24).

"I have spoken openly to the world," Jesus replied. "I always taught in synagogues or at the temple, where all the Jews come together. I said nothing in secret." (John 18:20)

"[King Agrippa] is familiar with these things, and I can speak freely to him. I [Paul] am convinced that none of this has escaped his notice, because it was not done in a corner." (Acts 26:26)

Are there times we should contact the secular media and times we should not? Absolutely! Feeding the homeless or providing basic necessities to victims of fire or climate devastations are compassionate ministries that would be difficult to interpret inappropriately. Church programs that help alleviate physical needs may be of interest to any local news media source. If so, Christ gets the glory!

Media is more than a community billboard; it is an avenue to reaching your community. Publicizing programs can emphasize the good work churches are doing, increase the influence of the local church, build credibility for your message, help shape opinions, and glorify God. Is your community glad the church is present and available?

What I Learned

- I learned to guard my words.

- I learned to encourage and utilize gifted people.

- I learned to be aware of major events affecting the community and nation.

- I learned to be open to opportunities allowing me to be a "voice for God."

- I learned I must inform the congregation of the Bible's instructions on moral issues.

Leadership Application

1. Politicians rise and fall by their public responses to crises. Go back over the past year and evaluate leadership responses to various church crises.

   a. What were the crises?

   b. What was the leadership's public response?

   c. What was the result of this response?

   d. What alternative responses can you list? Describe their disadvantages or merit.

2. What issues or concerns do you have with the news media?

3. What, in general, are the current issues churches need to be aware of? What resources do you consult for information?

4. Which way does the church you belong to lean: liberal or conservative? What are the most pronounced issues in this leaning?

5. What issues do you feel the church needs to be more relevant in handling? How might that be achieved?

6. Of the issues cited by the 2005 Student News Daily report, which ones are you the most sensitive to?

   a. Why?

b. How does the Bible influence your stance on that issue?

7. Write a 300-word letter to the editor describing the reasons for your concern and offer proactive alternatives to the issue of concern.

   a. How can your letter be a positive influence with people who "waver between two opinions" (1 Kings 18:21)?

   b. What objections would you anticipate? How would you answer them?

8. How will you achieve balance in the news resources you consult?

9. What preparations can your church make for "surprise visitors" who challenge your faith?

10. What concerns do you think Christians parents would have with the church's addressing sensitive issues in youth meetings? How can these concerns be mitigated?

Facing Death in the Congregation

"Randy, I have a friend in Norfolk General Hospital who has cancer, and it's terminal. Would you have time to visit her?" a church member asked.

"Of course. I'll go by tomorrow."

About 10 a.m. the next morning, I walked into her hospital room through an open door. NGH had recently remodeled this wing, and her room was spacious, newly painted, furnished with a couch and chairs as well as new equipment. The lights were turned off, and barely a sliver of sunlight crept in through the closed shades. She lay there with her head wrapped in bandages; tubes and wires stretched out to her arms and chest underneath her hospital gown.

I thought she might be asleep and gently tapped on the door. She opened her eyes and turned her head toward me. "Yes?" Her voice was weak, barely above a whisper.

I introduced myself. "Good morning, I'm Randy Childress, minister at Kempsville Christian Church in Virginia Beach. Carolyn Garrett is a member and asked me to check on you."

"Oh, hi!" she said. "Thanks for coming. I love Carolyn. She's so sweet. Come in."

I walked in and stood at the foot of her bed so she wouldn't have to strain her neck looking at me. She used the remote to raise the head of her bed, then with her arms pushed herself up to a near sitting position.

"How are you feeling this morning?" I asked. (I'd learned not to simply ask people how they were. They usually answered with an "OK" when they weren't. By asking how she was feeling *this morning*, I would get a definitive answer.)

"I'm weak this morning, Pastor."

"Please, call me Randy. That's what everybody at church calls me."

She gently smiled. "Randy."

"Do you hurt anywhere?" I asked.

She continued, "No. Oddly enough, nothing hurts me. I guess the pain medicine they give me is working."

"Are you able to sleep? Eat?"

"I sleep too much. What life I have is just slipping away. And I don't have an appetite. Anything I try to eat just makes me sick." She pointed to a tube stretching from an infusion bag to a needle in her arm. "They're feeding me this way."

It didn't take a genius to tell she was discouraged. We talked for a while until I sensed she was getting tired, and then I prepared to leave. I stood up and said, "Barbara, I'm glad I had the opportunity to get acquainted with you. I promise to keep you in prayer, but before I go, is there anything I can do for you?"

She looked down at the foot of her bed as if deciding whether or not to ask, then she looked up at me and said, "Can you tell me . . . what happens when we die?"

I sat down again, opened my pocket New Testament, and answered her questions from Scripture. Twenty minutes later, I was on the way back to the church office thinking, *Why do we wait so long to ask that question?*

That the Bible has the answer to the question "What happens at death?" obligates me to share it. The apostle Paul wrote,

> I do not want you to be unaware, brothers and sisters, that I planned many times to come to you (but have been prevented from doing so until now) in order that I might have a harvest among you, just as I have had among the other Gentiles. I am obligated both to Greeks and non-Greeks, both to the wise and the foolish. That is why I am so eager to preach the gospel also to you who are in Rome. (Romans 1:13–15)

The phrase "Nothing is certain except death and taxes" is generally attributed to Ben Franklin just after the writing of the Constitution of the United States. Yet it was the Bible that first stated, "People are destined to die once, and after that to face judgment" (Hebrews 9:27). If Jesus delays His coming, each of us are sure to face death.

Through service to the church, a minister faces death more often than most people, except for the funeral director and certain medical professionals. In forty-seven years of ministry I have conducted nearly 300 funerals. In this chapter I want to share with you the most memorable experiences I've had with church members as they passed.

The most difficult deaths

What is the most difficult type of death to deal with? Suicide. Without a doubt.

The phone rang several times early Friday morning. I barely got to it in time to answer. "Hello?" I said.

"Randy? This is Christy Adkins. How are you?"

"I'm great, Christy! Well, it's so good to hear from you. How are you?" Nearly fifteen years earlier, Christy had been one of the most active members in the youth group when I began ministry. Though only a teen herself, she had been responsible for much of my ministry there. She participated in all the activities, encouraged her friends to attend youth meetings with her, played the piano when we wanted to sing; she was a great help.

"I'm fine, thanks. Listen, I know you're getting ready to start your day, but I thought I should call. Trina is in the hospital."

"Trina?! What's wrong?" Trina was another girl who had been active in our group. She had embraced the nickname "Trina" because she was diminutive in statue—not extraordinarily so, but she was small for her age. She was precious to Sandi and me. If we could have, we would have adopted her all those years ago. This news was alarming.

"She cut her wrist, Randy. She tried to kill herself."

"Why?"

"I don't know, but I thought you should know."

I thanked Christy for calling, hung up the phone, and immediately Sandi and I prepared to make the 480-mile trip.

As we drove, Sandi and I discussed our memories of a sweet, vivacious, seven-year-old child. (That's how old she was when I started youth ministry.) When I left to begin a preaching ministry nearly one-hundred miles away, she was thirteen. Over the next five years, she and several other teens would drive the distance and visit with us. They had grown attached to our three sons and to us just as we had to them.

You couldn't find anyone more alive, more full of life than Trina was as a child. Always smiling, her bubbly personality was contagious. Sandi enjoyed having a little girl around and made a few dresses for her. Now, she was twenty-nine and married with a child of her own. She had a career, and graduated as a registered nurse. We could not understand how or why someone like Trina would try to end her life.

Suicide is the tenth leading cause of death in the US for all ages, that every day approximately 123 Americans die by their own hand— one person every twelve minutes. According to the Centers for Disease Control, suicide takes the lives of over 44,965 Americans every year and there is one suicide for every estimated twenty-five suicide attempts.[7]

What causes people to reach a point so low they no longer want to live? Dr. Alex Lickerman published an article in *Psychology Today* about suicide. According to Dr. Lickerman, there are six reasons people commit suicide. As you might expect, severe depression is first on the list. He points out, "depression warms their thinking, allowing ideas like, 'Everyone would be better off without me,' to make rational sense." Psychosis, perhaps from a chemical deficiency—a condition that could be manageable with medication—is listed second. Third is impulse, Dr. Lickerman suggests the result of drugs, alcohol, or burdening guilt. Finally, Dr. Lickerman goes on to list such causes as a "philosophical desire to die," "a mistake," and "the desire to be released from physical pain."[8] Which of these was Trina's reason?

We arrived that evening. I dropped Sandi and the kids off at my parents' house, then went directly to the hospital where Trina was still a patient. The door to her room was closed, so I gently knocked. There was no answer. I cracked the door an inch or two and called out, "Trina?"

A weakened, soft answer returned, "Yes?"

---

[7] "Suicide Facts," *Suicide Awareness Voices of Education*, accessed May 1, 2019, https://save.org/about-suicide/suicide-facts/.

[8] Alex Lickerman, M.D., "The Six Reasons People Attempt Suicide," *Psychology Today*, April 29, 2010, https://www.psychologytoday.com/us/blog/happiness-in-world/201004/the-six-reasons-people-attempt-suicide.

Then, I opened the door and stepped in. The room was about twenty feet long by fifteen feet wide. Directly across from the door was a large window that opened up to the mountain next to the hospital. From that window, all you could see were trees and brush, but there was life outside that window. Squirrels foraged for food, chipmunks scattered underneath the leaves from rock to rock, and birds fluttered from one branch to the other.

Trina's hospital bed had been pushed up next to the window. There she was, lying flat on her back. She turned to look at me.

"Hi," I smiled. "Remember me?"

Her eyes grew wide, then she turned her head away from me to face the window. I walked toward her.

"Trina . . . I heard you were in the hospital. Sandi and I came immediately. We just arrived."

Still no response from her.

"Trina . . . ?"

Then she started sobbing, her head still turned away from me. If I could have walked to the other side of the bed and looked her in the face, I would have, but the bed was too close to the wall. I pulled a chair up next to the bed and said, "Can you talk with me?"

Still no answer, her head still turned from me. Her muffled cry was now getting louder. I reached over to take her hand. She didn't pull away, but she raised her shoulder turning her back to me so I couldn't see her face.

"Trina, I've come a long way, just for you, won't you talk with me?" I paused. "We have to go back tomorrow morning. Will you look at me?"

No answer.

So I sat there talking to her, telling her about the ministry at Kempsville and what my boys were into now and recalling things the youth group did while I was her minister. She still wouldn't talk to me, and she wouldn't look toward me, but she never reclaimed her hand from mine. Instead, she gripped my hand firmly. She didn't want to face me, but she didn't want me to leave either. The more she cried, the more my heart broke.

After nearly an hour, with still no response from her, I decided to leave. I needed to be back at Kempsville for the Sunday morning service. She had calmed somewhat, but never once looked at me. I prayed with her and told her I would see her the next morning before we left.

The next morning, I walked to her door, and it was closed again. This time there was a sign on the door. "No Visitors," it said. I knocked on the door, and there was no answer. A nurse approached me and said, "It might be best to let her rest." I complied with the request, and we drove back to Virginia Beach hoping Trina would be all right in time. Over the next few days I tried to call, but to no avail. Unable to reach Trina or her husband, I hoped Trina had found the help she needed.

Two weeks later, Christy called again. Trina had attempted suicide again and this time succeeded. She was gone. If Christy knew what the problem was, she didn't reveal it. I hung up the phone and had to sit down. I was lost in my head. That's the only way to describe my emotions. Confused? Yes. Sad? Yes. But lost is the best way to describe it as my mind tried to search for a reason, moving from one possibility to another. *Why wasn't Trina able to talk to me? Didn't she trust me? What happened that would cause her to just give up and quit on life? Was she overwhelmed with guilt? Did I fail to teach her the grace of God? Did someone offend her to the point she didn't want to live anymore? Did I fail to teach her the strength available to her through the Holy Spirit?*

It has been nearly thirty years since her death and I still haven't recovered. Why did she feel suicide was her only way out? Why did she feel that she had no future to look forward to? If she had done wrong, why did she think her sin was greater than God's grace? Why did she believe that the world would be better without her? Why? Only God knows.

I've never been one to accept the teaching that suicide is a direct route to hell because it's the last sin committed without seeking repentance and forgiveness. That may be true for some, but others are overwhelmed with guilt, disappointment, and depression. David wrote, "Do not withhold your mercy from me, Lord; may your love and faithfulness always protect me. For troubles without number surround me; my sins have overtaken me, and I cannot see. They are more than the hairs of my head, my heart fails within me. Be pleased to save me, Lord; come quickly, Lord, to help me" (Psalm 40:11–13). David found strength in the Lord, but somehow Trina had missed that.

Despondent people can be so focused on their problems, they forget, or neglect, to look to God. We must continually remind people of His presence, His grace, and His power. "No temptation has overtaken you except what is common to mankind. And God is faithful; he will not let you be tempted beyond what you can bear. But when you are tempted, he will also provide a way out so that you can endure it" (1 Corinthians 10:13).

If Trina was lost because she died before repenting, we're all at risk. People die in accidents every day without opportunity to confess lies, forms of idolatry, or cheating.

God gives grace in spite of our weaknesses. Romans 8:38–39 says, "For I am convinced that neither death nor life, neither angels nor demons, neither the present nor the future, nor any powers, neither height nor depth, nor anything else in all creation, will be able to separate us from the love of God that is in Christ Jesus our Lord."

Trina never denied Christ. In a time of weakness, she momentarily lost sight of him (Ephesians 2:12). That doesn't mean He wasn't there, with her, reaching out to her. I remember the saying, "Christians aren't perfect; they're forgiven." I hope Trina is in heaven now realizing the mercy of God: "Who is a God like you, who pardons sin and forgives the transgression of the remnant of his inheritance. You do not stay angry forever but delight to show mercy" (Micah 7:18).

If we don't look to God as David did in his distress, we miss the resources He provides.

The most welcoming of deaths

"No, preacher, don't pray for me to get well. I'm ready to go."

What?!

Most people *want* me to pray for their recovery when ill, but not Jean. Jean was a sixty-three-year-old woman who had been in and out of hospitals for nearly twenty years. She had been married over forty years, had raised children and served her country. Inflicted with severe pain resulting in depression, Jean had lost any appetite for continued life in this world. She was a believer in Christ who had been faithful to church attendance and supported ministry programs at Kempsville; however, now she felt like retiring from life.

She was hospitalized when I visited her for the final time. She described her pain and told me what doctors were saying. I encouraged her not to give up. Before leaving, I took her hand and began praying. In my prayer I said, "Lord, I pray for encouragement and wisdom and healing for Jean." That was when she interrupted my prayer and said, "No, preacher, don't pray for me to get well. I'm ready to go home."

That statement caught me by surprise, so I simply prayed, "Lord, be with Jean, she's in your hands, your will be done." That night, the Lord took her home.

The sweetest death

"Randy, you better come now, they're turning off the machines tonight." That was the call from Sam about his wife's grandmother. Leona Bateman, a longtime member of our church, was eighty-nine years old when she faced death. She was short in stature but big in heart and long in influence. Her family was among the most close-knit families I knew.

When I walked into Mrs. Bateman's hospital room that evening, I found it to be filled with family members. She claimed two sons, three daughters, nineteen grandchildren, thirty-two great-grandchildren, and eight great-great-grandchildren. Except for the very youngest, I think nearly all of them were there crowded into her room, lined up against the wall. What I witnessed that night showed me the power of a mother's love.

Her heart was physically weak, but she was spiritually and emotionally strong. As she approached her last hours, her organs were shutting down. She had decided years before not to be kept alive by machines and put that decision in her living will. I walked over, took her hand, and said, "Mrs. Bateman, it's Randy."

She barely opened her eyes but acknowledged me with a nod of her head. I told her how much I appreciated her faithfulness to the church and to her family. Her lips curled up in a gentle smile. I prayed with her, asking the Lord to make her comfortable and give her peace. She gently squeezed my hand as I prayed.

I stood up and stepped out of the way when a nurse came in and started turning off and disconnecting the machines that kept her heart beating and fed her body. After that, the nurse maintained her vigil standing in the doorway. Everyone was quiet, watching, waiting to see what would happen and how soon it would happen. To everyone's surprise, Mrs. Bateman reached out toward her oldest daughter. Elizabeth cautiously approached, leaned down, and asked, "What is it, Mom? What is it?"

Mrs. Bateman puckered her lips and tried to raise up but was too weak. Elizabeth leaned down and kissed her mother. "Be at peace, Mom. I love you. Thank you for being so wonderful." She held her mother for a few moments, then said again, "I love you." She stood and backed out of the way, holding tissue to her mouth.

When she moved, the other daughters came, then the sons and grandchildren put their arms around her, each one kissing her and saying, "I love you." She puckered her lips for each kiss. This was the sweetest moment I had seen while in ministry. However, with each kiss, she grew weaker.

When everyone had said goodbye, they backed up around the walls of the room, holding hands or putting their arms around each other. No one spoke. Even the machines were silent now. It was quiet and peaceful as this family respectfully and lovingly waited for the passing of their mother.

Finally, she took her last breath. One by one the children looked to each other, then to the nurse. She checked Mrs. Bateman, then turned to the family and said, "She's gone." Grandchildren wept out loud and her children embraced each other. One by one they approached her bedside and kissed her again. Then they looked to me. I asked them to gather around the bed, hold hands, and pray with me. We prayed a simple but biblical prayer, "Lord, receive her spirit" (Acts 7:59).

The most trusting death

It was the most mournful, heartbreaking cry I had ever heard. I knew what Brad had just told Kathy. I also knew this was a very private moment between the two of them, but I couldn't sit still, I had to do something to try to help.

It was one o'clock in the afternoon, and I was doing research for an upcoming sermon. Printouts and books were scattered across my desk as I constructed the outline for my manuscript. I had closed the door, which had a glass panel in it, in hopes of privacy, but I could still see people walking by my office. They would smile and wave at me as they passed. My office was located directly across from the office of our small groups minister, and next to his was the office of our music director, Brad Mills. From my desk, I could see both offices. Kathy had just arrived. She looked my way and waved, then entered Brad's office.

Brad was a fifty-one-year-*young* man who had come to us from the west coast of Florida. I say "young" because he looked as if he were in his thirties. We had come across his name in the search for a music minister through a retired preacher friend of mine, Bob Shannon.

For one year, Bob had served a Florida church as interim minister while they searched for a lead pastor. I had called Bob asking if he knew anyone who might fit our music department, and he gave me Brad's name. "He and his wife are both very personable. You'll like them." I contacted Brad, he submitted his resume, and we decided to bring him to Virginia Beach for an interview. Bob was right; we immediately liked them both.

Dark hair, piercing dark eyes, tall, and athletic, Brad had an outgoing personality. Sandi and I took both Brad and Kathy to dinner to get acquainted and were impressed right away. "Oh, they're so cute!" Sandi said. "They seem so happy together."

Brad had not gone to Bible college, and he had no formal training in music, so I was interested in why he wanted to go into worship ministry. In our conversation I learned he had taught himself to read music and could play a piano proficiently. At the time, he owned a photography studio in Florida, but his first love was the Lord, his second love was Kathy, and his third love was Christian music. He wanted to spend the rest of his life leading people in praise to God, he said.

Upon hiring him, we were pleased to find that whatever Brad lacked in musical training was made up for in personality and leadership skills. Over the years he was with us, he directed choirs, quartets, trios, and solos. He started a praise band, chose the music, and made the arrangements for each instrument, and he tackled the most difficult job of supervising *Living Pictures*, a musical dramatization of the life of Christ involving over one hundred people in the cast and crew.

Friendly and supportive, Brad also became a living link between offices. At least once a week, he would call the staff into my office "just to fellowship," which looked like talking sports and laughing over coffee. Brad had laugh that was contagious, and we loved to hear it. If he heard a joke, he would laugh out loud, and his laugh was funnier than the joke. When he laughed, we laughed with him. Often Brad would meet a couple of us to play tennis or golf too. He kept up with baseball, football (Tampa Bay, of course), auto racing, and professional tennis. He loved life and people.

We also gained a valuable asset in Kathy on their arrival. Kathy immediately jumped in to help Brad. She joined the choir, helped organize the music material for ministry, and made "reminder calls." She actively participated in the women's ministry and made friends quickly. Her bright personality uplifted every group she participated in.

Kathy had retired from a major airline as a flight attendant, which probably explained her outgoing personality and charm. She was accustomed to meeting and dealing with people, all kinds of people. Happy passengers, demanding passengers, or angry passengers, she knew how to appease them all. That, in itself, was a wonderful personality trait.

Kathy was also trained to calm anxious passengers on a delayed flight, nervous, frightened passengers on a bumpy flight, or difficult passengers who had gotten out of control for whatever reason. Her training had paid off often during the course of her career.

She had comforted and encouraged others, but now she would need that herself.

For me, it started one Tuesday when, after a staff meeting, we decided to go to lunch at a local restaurant. There was a buffet bar, and when Brad sat next to me at the table, I was amazed at how much food he had put on his plate.

"Brad!" I said. "How do you eat all that and stay so slim?"

Brad chuckled, busying himself with his plate. "I don't know," he answered. "I guess I just burn it off. Workin' hard, ya know?" We would learn later his body was fighting a battle.

The next Tuesday in the staff meeting, we closed by asking for prayer requests. Brad said, "You know, I've got this lump in my stomach. I'm going to get it checked out today. Keep me in your prayers." He returned that afternoon telling us the doctor had ordered a battery of tests. We didn't like the sound of that but assumed it was standard procedure for anything suspicious.

In the following weeks, Brad went to the hospital for a series of blood tests and physical exams. X-rays, CT scans, and MRIs were ordered. He was exhausted from all the grueling procedures. It seemed the more tests they put him through, the more tests they wanted to conduct.

Two days after his last test, the oncologist contacted him and reported Brad had tested positive for non-Hodgkin's lymphoma. NHL is a cancer of the lymphatic system that produces tumors in the body. This must have been what Brad felt in his lower abdomen. The tumor could be fast-growing, so treatment would have to be aggressive. I knew Brad to be mentally tough, but I wondered how *Kathy* would receive the news.

Through a series of chemotherapy treatments, Brad lost a considerable amount of weight and lost hair on his scalp and eyebrows; yet throughout, he did not lose that pleasant, upbeat personality. He continued to work in the music ministry, only missing a couple of worship services and practices. In spite of the ordeal he went through, he continued to laugh, to encourage and motivate people, never letting them see discouragement or depression. Whatever came to him, he would maintain a witness of faith, trusting in God. He would, however, share his feelings with those who were closest to him: Josh, our small groups minister; Bill, a deacon and member of the choir; and me. Even when talking with us, he never showed fear or dread, only concern for Kathy.

I will always remember the solo he sang one Sunday morning in our worship service. Having lost all his hair, he stood on the platform dressed in a suit that was now a size or two too large for him, holding a microphone to his mouth and singing "My Tribute."

Just let me live my life, let it pleasing, Lord to Thee.[1]

Throughout the weeks and months as Brad fought cancer, Kathy had been a source of strength. She had determined to be upbeat and motivating for her husband. With all he had to go through, she didn't want Brad to worry about her, but the pressure and frustration was growing within her. She depended heavily upon her devotional prayer life. Still, she was confused. *Why this? Why now? He has just dedicated his whole life to God's service.* She continued to immerse herself into Bible study and prayer, following Brad's example to be a strong witness for Christ. She continued in the women's ministry at church, writing notes, making calls, and encouraging other women.

On this day, however, she came by the office to get the latest test results and learned the doctor had called to say treatments weren't working. At first, she looked blankly at Brad, then months of turbulent emotions began to pour out. She stood by Brad's desk and wept. He went to her and gently, lovingly wrapped his arms around her. The longer she stood there, the more pain she felt. She let it all out.

I was startled at first when I heard her cry. I sat back and looked toward his office, intending to let them alone, but her mournful cry broke my heart. It echoed throughout the hallways of the church building. Machines stopped, the clicking of computer keys stopped, phone conversations paused; the building grew silent, and the only sound was Kathy's sobbing. Her loving husband, her best friend, was terminally ill. All her efforts, all her hopes of healing, collapsed with a heart-wrenching moan.

I dropped my pen and put my head down on my desk. Closing my eyes, I prayed for them both. "Lord, only you can minister to them at this time. Please help. Dear God, please."

She continued to cry, and I could not sit still. It was too much for me; I had to *do* something. I entered Brad's office to see them standing there. He was comforting Kathy in his arms while she sobbed. Neither of them

---

[1] Andraé Crouch, "My Tribute," 1972.

acknowledged me, but I went to them, placed my arms around them, and said, "Kathy, it's going to be all right. You'll be okay." It was the only thing I knew to do at the moment, but it wasn't enough as she continued to cry. I don't think she heard me or even knew I was there. Brad stood there tall and straight. He was strong for her. He continued to hold her, patiently rocking her side to side. "Shhh, baby. Shhh, shhh, I love you. Shhh." Later, I thought to myself, *Brad stood there like a rock*, and I admired his courage and strength. I left them and returned to my office knowing only the Holy Spirit could help them now.

I had seen couples undergo these circumstances before in my years of ministry. I thought of another devoted couple who had received nearly the same diagnosis. She also cried when doctors reported treatments weren't working. One day when I visited them in the hospital, I learned he was declining rapidly. She asked me to step out in the hallway to talk. She said, "I'm doing all I know to do. What else can I do?"

As she talked, I realized she blamed herself for her husband's deterioration and thought she had failed him and failed God. When she told me that, I said, "What on earth made you think *that*?"

She looked both ways to see if anyone would hear. "I told myself, 'This is a test,'" she said, "and I thought if I tried hard, if I did right, I would pass the test and he would be healed." She had to catch her breath to keep from crying.

I looked at this grieving woman. She was disappointed and broken, blaming herself for her husband's illness. She didn't think she was good enough to earn God's favor. "Oh, no," I said, "you're not to blame for your husband's cancer. Sickness and death are the result of living in a sin-stained, imperfect world where there are germs, viruses, and diseases. Your husband isn't sick because you didn't believe God enough. Please don't think that. Sickness and death eventually comes to all of us. The question is, will you lean on God and trust Him to sustain you through this? That's the test, and *you haven't failed it yet.*"

I wrote down a number of Scripture passages for her to read and pray over in the coming days. The following week, I called to check on her and she had calmed down. She expressed gratitude for the church's ministry to her family. She concluded by saying, "I'm leaning on God with all my weight."

I don't think Kathy blamed herself *or* blamed God. I don't even think she was afraid of being alone without Brad. But I think she was overwhelmed with all the treatments and disappointments as she thought about what pain her husband would go through, and she was brokenhearted that they would be separated for a while, maybe for years. I knew Kathy's faith was substantial. It was strong. She believed in Jesus, and she knew she and Brad would eventually meet again in heaven.

A few weeks later, Josh, my son and the Small Groups Leader and I had the day off and were playing golf. We were on the seventh fairway, when a call came through to his phone. Brad was at the clinic receiving more chemo and wasn't feeling good. We weren't sure how to interpret this message, so we returned our cart to the clubhouse and went to the clinic to be with him.

We were led back into a large room with a number of people receiving treatments and medical personnel walking around. My first thought was of how there was no privacy. I realized later, these cancer patients had become acquainted with each other and provided support to one another.

At the far end of the room, Brad and Kathy sat next to the window, Brad with his feet spread apart and a bucket between them. The chemo was making him violently ill. He began telling us what the doctors had reported, that so far the chemo was still having no effect but that they wanted to continue the treatments. Kathy was exhausted and took a break while we were there to get some coffee. She knew Brad would be more comfortable talking openly to us alone.

"Doesn't look like treatments are going to work, fellas," he said. "The cancer is growing and spreading throughout my body."

"Brad, do you hurt anywhere?" I asked.

"I don't really have any severe pain, just some discomfort right here." He pulled up his shirt to show us a lump on his stomach. "These treatments have sapped me of energy. I'm tired all the time, and I have no appetite." Then he looked toward the door Kathy had exited. "Poor Kathy. She has to put up with all this. If I don't eat, she refuses to eat."

As we talked on, Josh told the latest antics of his three kids and Brad made light of his treatments. His laughter rang throughout the large room. It was an unusual treat for nurses and workers. They looked back to him and smiled, not accustomed to hearing much laughter in that room.

One afternoon, I visited Brad and Kathy in their home. Their living room was beautifully decorated with a couch and three chairs with tables interspersed between them. Large prints from Brad's photography studio adorned the walls. Formal pictures from their wedding and strategically arranged photo prints of the two of them together were also displayed. Those prints were like a photo journal showing places they had been and things they had done. But the most obvious feature: they showed two people happy and in love.

Brad, wearing a sweatsuit—not for exercise but for warmth—and tennis shoes, sat on the couch while Kathy sat opposite me in one of the chairs. He had decided we needed to talk over some issues, the most difficult issues that had consumed his thoughts in the past few weeks. Having done all he could do for his health, Brad now wanted to set the music ministry at Kempsville in order.

First, he wanted to recommend his own replacement, Dan Kline, someone very much like himself. "Dan has a solid faith, and he loves contemporary Christian music," Brad said. "He is extremely talented, and he can help make the transition to a contemporary service." He sighed. "I always hoped to be the one to start the contemporary service . . ." He turned to me, more upbeat. "Anyway, Dan plays practically every instrument in a band. He'll be a good fit, and you'll like him." (We found Brad's estimation of Dan's talents to be right.)

After talking about the music program, Brad brought up his passing and final arrangements. Kathy fidgeted and repositioned herself in her chair. "I don't want a sad service," he said. "If what I have been doing here has helped people love the Lord, then that's what we ought to do . . . love the Lord in praise and worship! I want a celebration service, not a service with a few praise songs. I want people to celebrate, stand, and clap their hands—you know, be *joyful* in the Lord!"

From then on, we never talked about a funeral but instead a celebration of life service. There would be lots of music. It would, of course, include "My Tribute" as one of the songs.

"Brad," I said, "just be honest with me. How are you feeling about all this? How are you handling it all?"

Brad lifted his hands, and his bare eyebrows, to explain, "Honestly, Randy, I'm at peace with it all. I mean, we *all* gotta die sometime or other, don't we?"

I nodded.

"Well . . . so I go before you." He paused and looked at his wife. "My only regret is that I leave Kathy."

I thought about this for a moment, then said, "You know, Brad, there's no time in heaven. Eternity is not measured in hours, weeks, months, or years." I let that sink in. "No sooner than you get there, you'll turn around and see me, you'll see Kathy. For you, time will be no more."

His eyes widened, "Well, that's right, isn't it?" He turned to Kathy. "I'll see you before you know it."

Kathy, sitting in her chair facing Brad, her eyes welling up with tears, smiled and nodded. She went over and sat next to him, curled her arm around his arm, and took his hand in hers, their fingers interlocked. He smiled back at her and gripped her hand firmly.

"Easy there, buster," she exclaimed. "I've only got two hands, and that's my best one."

Thinking I was imposing, I cleared my throat and said, "Brad, is there anything I can do for you before I leave?"

He turned toward me. "Well, yeah . . ." Softly now, "Tell me what's going to happen?"

"When you pass?"

He nodded.

"Brad, all I can tell you is what the Bible says."

"That's all I want, Randy."

I took a deep breath and prayed a quick prayer. *Lord, help me here.*

"Okay, first off, the Bible teaches that if Jesus delays His coming, we *all* will die," I said. Brad nodded, and Kathy put her other hand over his.

"And, when Jesus told the parable of the rich man and Lazarus, he said the angels carried Lazarus to Abraham's side. That tells me that Christ won't let us go through this alone; angels will meet us and accompany us to heaven." Brad nodded again while Kathy stroked his arm. Without saying a word, she comforted and strengthened him.

I continued, "As I understand it, they'll take us right into the presence of Christ. We'll see Him in glory.[2] He will *personally* welcome us. Brad, that's so powerful a thought I can't even describe it, but He will give us the inheritance He purchased for us on the cross. And we'll enjoy that forever."

Brad looked down at his hands and said thoughtfully, "He'll say, 'Well done, good and faithful servant. Enter into the joy of the Lord.'" Even though he knew everything I was saying, somehow it seemed to do him

---

[2] Matthew 25:31–40.

good to hear it all again. I admired this man's courage and faith in the midst of his suffering.

"Right." I went on. "There will be opportunities for us to be productive, for we'll serve the Lord without any physical limitations.[3] Think of it, productivity . . . our weaknesses here won't limit us there. Our lack of knowledge won't limit us. We'll be productive without limitation." I paused and looked at my music minister. "I might even be able to get into the choir."

Brad laughed, because he knew I can't sing on key. "Not if I'm directing!" he said.

Brad thought for a moment, then, "Randy, I know the Bible says we won't be married in heaven . . ." It was an awkward question. He looked toward Kathy. "But will we know each other?"

"Yes, I'm convinced of that. Jesus *did* say, 'At the resurrection people will neither marry nor be given in marriage; they will be like the angels in heaven.'[4] But the Bible *does* indicate we'll know each other. Even though we haven't received our resurrection bodies yet [we will when Christ comes back], we'll know each other. The book of Revelation says John acknowledged there were people present in heaven. Not vaporous beings, but *people* . . . people who had previously lived physically, materially on earth.[5]

"Not only that, but in the Old Testament, when king Saul hired the witch of Endor to call up the departed spirit of the prophet Samuel, both she and Saul recognized Samuel. And when Jesus was transfigured before Peter, James, and John, the disciples recognized Moses and Elijah who had died hundreds of years before they were born.

---

[3] Revelation 7:13–15; 22:3.
[4] Matthew 22:30.
[5] Revelation 7:9.

"I don't need to *see* Sandi to recognize her voice," I said. "And sometimes when I don't see or hear her, I sense her presence. In heaven, we'll have greater sense and awareness. Heaven won't dull our senses; we'll be smarter in heaven, not slower. The apostle Paul wrote, 'For now we see only a reflection as in a mirror; then we shall see face to face. Now I know in part; then I shall know fully, even as I am fully known' [1 Corinthians 13:12]. We'll be smarter, more aware. Our senses in heaven will be unlimited."

Kathy spoke up. "Randy, I know heaven is a place of joy, but what about family members and friends that aren't there? How can we rejoice knowing they didn't make it to heaven?"

"No, there won't be sorrow in heaven [Revelation 21:4]. Heaven won't allow it."

Kathy was puzzled. "But if we're smarter, how can we *not* know, and if we know they're not in heaven, how can we not *help* but be sad?"

I thought about this for a moment and then said, "It's not easy to explain, but if you can, think of a moment when you experienced joy or exhilaration so wonderful, so intense, that no worry or bad thought came to your mind—maybe on an amusement park ride or while having dinner with friends. It was so enjoyable that you didn't think about worries or troubles."

Brad's eyebrows went up as he looked at Kathy. "I can certainly think of one." She blushed, slapped his arm, and looked back at me.

"Well," I cleared my throat, "if you *can* imagine such a moment, that's sorta what heaven will be like for all eternity. There's no time in heaven, so you would live in that moment forever, with no sorrow, no regret."

A lull came in the conversation, and Brad was looking tired, so I had prayer with them and let myself out while the two of them sat together on the couch.

Over the next few weeks, Brad's cancer started causing pain. Doctors gave him analgesics followed by even stronger medicines, which confined him to bed. Kathy had a hospital bed placed in their den so she could be with him twenty-four seven. Close friends at church took turns sitting with him so she could take a nap now and then to catch up on sleep she missed watching Brad through the night.

On one evening I sat with Brad, the pain medicine made him restless; it had him tossing and turning in his bed. I was seated by the bed while Kathy stood at the foot of the bed. All her emotions welled up inside her again, and she started to cry. Brad hadn't spoken for some time. We assumed the pain medicine was keeping him quiet. But then he started trying to climb over the bed rail, threatening to pull out a tube from his arm. I had to pull him back, but he resisted me. By now he was weakened, but still he was determined to get over the rail. I'm heavier and had to place my hands on his shoulders to keep him from raising up and getting leverage.

Kathy became frightened for him. "Why is he doing that?" she asked.

I looked at Brad and noticed his eyes were laser-focused on Kathy.

"He wants to comfort you," I said.

I took my hands off him. Kathy walked to the other side of the bed and leaned over to kiss his cheek, and Brad reached both arms around her and held her. No words were spoken by either of them. Even today, years later, I think this is the sweetest picture of a loving husband and wife I have seen. I took that as a hint and left the two of them embracing each other in that powerful demonstration of love.

A few nights later, I received a call from Bill East, one of Brad and Kathy's close friends who had taken a turn to sit with Brad. "I think you better come," he said. "I don't think it will be long."

I gently knocked on the door, and Bill opened it to let me in. He didn't say anything but led me back to the den where Brad lay and Kathy sat in a chair by his side, holding his hand. Brad's breathing had become shallow and intermittent. The pauses between breaths were lengthening. For several minutes Bill stood on one side and Kathy and I stood on the other. Kathy continued holding Brad's hand, massaging it. We didn't talk; we simply listened for the sounds of his breaths. With each breath he took, we wondered . . .

Finally, he exhaled. We waited for the next breath, but it didn't come. One second, three seconds, ten seconds, it never came.

Kathy threw herself across Brad's chest, sobbing. Bill and I stayed at our posts by the bed. I placed my hand on Kathy's back and patted between her shoulders; Bill reached down to put his hand on her shoulder.

After a few moments, I leaned down, my face parallel to hers, and said, "Kathy, he was a great friend and brother to me. If there's one thing I know for sure, he loved you. In the years I worked with him, I never saw anything or heard him say anything inappropriate to make me think otherwise. I never doubted he loved you."

Kathy, now resting across Brad's chest, turned her head toward me, smiled broadly, and said, "I know."

I have often remembered those two words: *I know.* How wonderful that at this moment a wife knew the love of her husband, without *any* doubts.

A week later, a celebration service to remember Brad Mills was held on a Friday evening. I preached a message, and the service was joyful with many praise songs. Our 800-seat worship center was nearly full as church members and friends who came to honor Brad celebrated his life. To God be the glory!

Psalm 150

Praise the Lord.

Praise God in his sanctuary;

praise him in his mighty heavens.

Praise him for his acts of power;

praise him for his surpassing greatness.

Praise him with the sounding of the trumpet,

praise him with the harp and lyre,

praise him with timbrel and dancing,

praise him with the strings and pipe,

praise him with the clash of cymbals,

praise him with resounding cymbals.

Let everything that has breath praise the Lord.

Praise the Lord.

What I Learned

- I learned to emphasize God's grace to His children.

- I learned that by saying to Peter, "Feed my sheep," Jesus was instructing preachers like me to teach His children how to survive and thrive in the Christian life.

- I learned there comes a point when people welcome death.

- I learned I must teach people to be unafraid of death, to view it as a doorway to heaven.

- I learned to teach people God has a purpose for each life and to live that purpose out until God calls us home.

- I learned death is God's call, not my own.

- I learned my most effective influence can be felt at the loss of a loved one.

- I learned funeral messages can become an opportunity to glorify God and lead people to Christ.

- I learned real strength is not measured in the size of our muscles but in the depth of our faith.

- I learned to discover all I can about helping people through terminal illness.

- I learned to create a file containing excerpts from sermons appropriate for funeral messages.

Leadership Application

1. Do you know anyone who committed suicide? How did you feel when you received the news?

2. How do you want to be remembered at *your* funeral service?

3. What matters do you think should be covered in a living will?

4. What counsel would you give to someone faced with terminal illness?

5. What is your opinion about machinery that keeps people alive?

6. Of the reasons people commit suicide listed by Dr. Lickerman, other than depression, which do you think is the most common? What would you say to a person experiencing that?

7. What resources does God provide to sustain us . . .

    a. as we face death?

    b. as we face the loss of a loved one?

8. How do you help a person dealing with guilt or regret after the loss of a loved one?

9. Have you ever been to a funeral service that was uplifting and encouraging? What were the features that made it so?

Virtue: Personal Responsibility

The most difficult chapter in this book.

In more than forty-five years of ministry, there has only been one instance when I thought maybe a woman other than my wife might possibly have designs on me. I was in my early thirties, serving a small church in the country where everyone knew everyone else. Even though many of the members worked in the local factory, it was a farming community, and the church had a slow, easygoing, laid-back atmosphere to it. It was like a neighborhood of friends who trusted each other enough to leave their doors unlocked.

The office staff consisted of myself and a seventy-something-year-old lady named Ruth. Ruth had never married but had dedicated her adult years to the care of her invalid mother. By this time, her mother had passed and she lived alone. Ruth had a strong personality. She was forthright and often blunt and outspoken. Some people found it difficult to get along with her, but Sandi and I connected with her almost immediately. She was very kind and supportive of my ministry, and she was there when I needed her.

I received a call one morning from a new member, a young woman about my age. Laura had joined the church a month earlier, joined the choir, and made friends very quickly. She had something she wanted to discuss and wanted to know if we could meet. However, the only time she had available was late afternoon . . . after Ruth went home. It was common knowledge in the church that Ruth's hours were 8 a.m. to 2 p.m. After we finished our phone conversation, I went to Ruth and asked her if she would be willing to stay a couple of extra hours to be in the building while I met with Laura. She agreed and busied herself with typing the next newsletter.

The first meeting with Laura was a pleasant one. She told me how glad she was to find a church she could call home. She enjoyed singing in the choir and wanted to know what other programs I could recommend for her involvement. We talked about some of the ministries going on and after about a half hour, she left. I thanked Ruth for staying. "No problem," Ruth said, "It's good you have someone else in the building. I can be here anytime." Looking back, I believe Ruth had a sense about Laura that made her uncomfortable.

The next week, Laura called and asked if we could meet again. This time, however, the only time she could meet was 7:00 p.m. Knowing the building would be empty, I hesitated, but she said, "Please. I need to talk." I remembered Ruth had said she was available anytime, so I agreed. After hanging up the phone, I went into Ruth's office and asked if she could come back at 6:45 and stay while Laura and I met. She graciously agreed.

If she was surprised to see Ruth when she arrived, Laura didn't show it. She walked into my office and asked if she could close the door. I said yes. Then, after a few words of greeting, she got right to the point. She was attracted to men. She hesitated and stared at me waiting for a response. "Okay," I said uncomfortably, "most girls are." She smiled and told me her problem: it didn't matter to her if the men were married. In fact, she told me she often met men at the local airport. *Uh oh . . . why is she telling me this?* Maybe I was naïve, but I was shocked at the idea.

Everything about this meeting made me uncomfortable. The subject of the conversation alone made me feel awkward, but the way she stared directly at me, as if poring through my head, trying to read my thoughts, unflinching, disturbed me.

Finally, I asked, "What is it you want to get out of this meeting, Laura? Why tell me this?"

She shrugged. "I don't know . . . Well, you're my preacher . . . I just thought you should know."

"Well, obviously, you know what you're doing is wrong." I tried to say that calmly but firmly.

"Yes, I know." *Finally,* she looked away.

I didn't feel qualified to attempt a counseling session with her and offered to make contact with a Christian counselor. I wanted to end this meeting quickly and direct her to someone better trained to deal with such things. However, she wasn't comfortable, she said, sharing this with anyone else. "It was difficult enough telling *you,* let alone some stranger."

I quoted a number of scriptures to her, and she nodded her head acknowledging each passage. If *I* didn't have a good answer for her I was hoping the Word of God would convict and convince her to repent.

She left, and I went in to Ruth's office thanking her again for putting in the extra time. She didn't mind at all. Ruth often had an expression on her face that said she was wise to the situation, any situation. She had that expression then. As I drove home, I thought maybe Laura would get control of her behavior.

A few weeks later, she started showing up to the office at various times, bringing gifts to me and my sons. Ruth didn't like it and didn't receive her in a friendly manner. After a while, she started driving out to our house several miles from the church building delivering gifts. I became more and more uncomfortable with her attention, so I talked to Sandi without betraying Laura's admission. Then I asked Laura to stop bringing gifts and showing up so often. Of course she was offended and started attending a different church. Five months later I learned the minister resigned due to a moral indiscretion. I never learned if Laura was involved, but I thought to myself, even ministers are at risk.

Some people might accuse me of an irrational, paranoid insensitivity, say I should have been more patient, encouraging her in her Christian life. I did, in fact, read scripture and pray with her in our meetings, but I felt she needed someone more capable than me, a professional counselor. I believe Ruth could have done more good for her than I.

If, in fact, she did have designs on me, her efforts were doomed to failure because I was married in the strongest sense of the word. I love my wife intensely and would not dare do anything to jeopardize my marriage or my relationships with my three sons. Today, after forty-seven years of marriage, Sandi is still the sweetest and most beautiful person I know.

I am so glad I didn't do anything stupid, for that reason as well as three others. First, I was devoted to my ministry and setting an example for the church. These people had been through a difficult, tumultuous time before I arrived, and an error on my part could have set them back for years. Second, my parents' love for each other had made a lasting impression upon me, and I didn't want to do anything to disappoint them. Finally, and most importantly, I knew God was there with me.

I remember an older minister talking to me about temptation. He wasn't particularly talking about sexual temptation but anything that could lead us into sin. He said, "Remember temptation to disobey God comes from the devil or a weak flesh, probably both. When we're tempted, it's not that we don't believe in God anymore; it's that we're so distracted by the temptation at the moment that we forget Him." He went on to give the example of Joseph, when Potiphar's wife tried to tempt him. "What did Joseph do?" he said. "I'll tell you what he did—he ran! And as he ran, he said, 'How can I commit this sin *against God*?' He was in such close fellowship with God that when he was tempted, Joseph couldn't forget God was there with him."

Still, like Joseph, each of us must admit vulnerability and constantly take precautions. In the building of the next church I ministered to, we replaced the office doors with doors that had glass in them and instituted a policy that staff members could not counsel when no one else was present in the building. News reports were making it clear to us that we needed preventive methods. However, glass in doors does not control what two people say to each other or prevent plans they might make in privacy.

The rate of sexual abuse and infidelity is shocking! One study by the University of Washington, Seattle of over 19,000 people revealed infidelity among men had risen from 20% to 28% in a fifteen-year period. During that same period, rates of infidelity by women increased from 5% to 15%.[1] *Increased* is the important word.

In a study of the life of David, Dallas Theological Seminary professor Howard Hendricks revealed the results of a study he conducted of 246 men who had been in full-time ministry and experienced moral failure. He reported, "More than 80% of the men became sexually involved with the other woman after spending significant time with her, often in counseling situations. Without exception, each of the 246 men had been convinced that sort of fall 'would never happen to me.'"[2]

As I write this, the Catholic Church has just released the names of priests who allegedly committed sexual abuse while serving in Virginia.[3] And this same week, major newspapers in Texas published articles describing the failure of Southern Baptist churches to prevent sexual abuse in their congregations due to the autonomy (self-government) of the Southern Baptist Convention.[4]

In a 2011 article on Crosswalk.com, Dr. Chet Weld points to a study that reveals 10% of all psychologists have had an affair with a client, while 30% of all pastors have had an affair with a member of the congregation. He accounts for the difference with the *preventive* training psychologists

---

[1] Tara Parker-Pope, "Love, sex and the changing landscape of infidelity," *The New York Times*, October 28, 2008, https://www.nytimes.com/2008/10/28/health/28iht-28well.17304096.html.

[2] Garret Kell, "The Pattern Among Fallen Pastors," *The Gospel Coalition*, May 26, 2015, https://www.thegospelcoalition.org/article/the-pattern-among-fallen-pastors/.

[3] Bridget Balch, "Virginia's Catholic dioceses name 50 priests accused of child sex abuse," *Richmond Times-Dispatch*, February 13, 2019, https://www.richmond.com/news/virginia/virginia-s-catholic-dioceses-name-priests-accused-of-child-sex/article_b47be8e9-6f7f-596e-9ed0-6927292b2d5d.html.

[4] Robert Downen, Lise Olsen, and John Tedesco, "Abuse of Faith," *Houston Chronicle*, February 10, 2019, https://www.houstonchronicle.com/news/investigations/article/Southern-Baptist-sexual-abuse-spreads-as-leaders-13588038.php

receive. According to Weld, psychologists take a course in ethics that teaches them "how to draw boundaries with clients; how to seek counseling for themselves, how to avoid temptations in the office, how to make appropriate referrals, learning professional consequences of inappropriate behavior, grasping the importance of 'doing no harm' to a client, learning about the requirement to report another psychologist that you hear about that's having an affair, and other ethical and legal teachings."

Weld writes, "I've had two years of seminary and three years of Bible College, and I never took such a course."[5] This article is dated 2011. Hopefully Christian schools have updated their course studies to include this training.

In response to the crisis reported among Southern Baptists, J.D. Greear, president of the Southern Baptist Convention, in 2019 proposed "providing more resources for churches to deal with sexual abuse, requiring more background checks for leaders and staff, and changing the SBC bylaws to allow for the removal of churches that show a 'wanton disregard for sexual abuse.' He also announced in an agreement by the six Southern Baptist seminaries to make training on abuse prevention mandatory."[6]

The solution is personal responsibility

In other chapters I have tried to demonstrate the adventure and thrill of ministry. These chapters have largely had good conclusions. However, there are challenges, significant challenges, to every ministry, not just in the minister's own life but in the life of the congregation as well. Church leaders, teachers, and other influencers must be aware of weaknesses in the human personality.

---

[5] Dr. Chet Weld, "Pastoral Infidelity: Problems and Solutions," Crosswalk. com (blog), December 26, 2011, https://www.crosswalk.com/church/pastors-or-leadership/pastoral-infidelity-problems-and-solutions.html.

[6] Kiley Crossland, "SBC leader proposes reforms to address sexual abuse," *World News Group*, February 19, 2019, https://world.wng.org/content/sbc_leader_proposes_reforms_to_address_sexual_abuse.

When a church leader commits an indiscretion, the damage hits scores of people, extending even beyond church membership. As a church leader I see myself as a protector and caretaker of members' souls. As a preacher, I see myself as a disseminator of God's Word, lovingly applying it where needed.

The following events occurred over a number of years and in different churches where I served as minister. You may or may not be pleased with my responses to them, but at least you'll have the opportunity to strategize your responses. I'm not happy with the way I handled them, nor am I happy with the end results, but I share them now hoping this report will help church members and leaders become more aware of possible compromises to ministry and the need to prepare for remediation.

*****

Over the years, and in various churches, I've been forced to deal with infidelity among members and staff. For example, a divorced man at one church took interest in a married woman whose husband did not attend with her. The first time I noticed them together, they were talking together in the hallway between services. There was nothing out of the ordinary about that except they were very attentive to each other, and the same happened for a few weeks after. Often they seemed to slide off to the side of the hallway, impervious to the presence of others, as not to be interrupted. Not long after that, they were sitting together in worship. They grew more and more familiar with each other in public, so I decided to talk to the man. He agreed to meet with me in my office one Sunday afternoon while committees and ministry teams were meeting throughout the building. I think he assumed we would talk about a particular program he was involved in. We sat at a small table I used for conferences. After a brief conversation:

"Wayne, I wanted to talk with you about Jennifer."

A look of surprise came over his face.

I went on. "It seems the two of you are getting closer than you should."

"What do you mean?"

"I mean, you're always together. I never see you with other people. It's like a bond is developing between the two of you."

Wayne looked at the table. "Jennifer is a sweet person. I enjoy being around her . . ." Then he looked up at me. "Why is that any of *your* business?"

"It's my business because I see a dangerous trend developing. Let me tell you what this looks like. This looks like the two of you are developing an inappropriate relationship. It's my business because it's happening on church property. She's *married*, Wayne!" Then I said, "I'm asking you to keep your distance."

Wayne took his forefinger and began poking at the table. "Look, Randy, she's not happy. Her marriage is falling apart anyway. The guy she's married to is a bum!"

"I already know they're struggling, but if their marriage does fall apart, *you* shouldn't be one of the reasons. I don't want you to contribute to a breakup. As long as they're married, you shouldn't be a factor. Back away and give them the space they need to resolve their problems."

Wayne exploded. He jumped up, kicking his chair back, took hold of the table between us, and flipped it over. I stood up and jumped back to avoid it. Wayne stormed out the door, and I followed him to see several people in the hallway startled by the noise.

Jennifer and her husband did separate and eventually divorced. I wasn't able to get in touch with either of them or with Wayne.

*****

In another instance, a businessman invited me to lunch. "I have something I want to talk over with you."

"I'm always good for lunch," I said, and then we made an appointment. I wondered what it could be. He was a successful businessman, an engineer, who had bought a small farm and kept a couple of horses. Sometimes businessmen were excited about a new project and wanted me to pray with them. Had it been for friendship, I would have been delighted with that too. He was very personable.

We sat at the table talking college football, farming, and business enterprises he had in mind. Then I opened the discussion further. "Brian, you said you had something to talk with me about."

Brian adjusted himself in his chair and leaned forward with his elbows on the table and hands clasped. He looked like a supervisor about to deliver bad news. He cleared his throat and lowered his voice. "Yeah, uh, Randy . . . for the last couple of years Becky and I haven't been happy."

"Oh?" This genuinely surprised me. Brian, Becky, and their two children were regular attenders. When they were at the church building, theirs looked like a model marriage. Becky played the piano for worship and taught a Wednesday evening Bible study for children.

Brian continued. "Yes, and I wanted you to know that . . . well, I'm going to move out and get my own place."

"Oh no, Brian! How long have you and Becky been married?"

"Next June will make ten years, but I don't know if you can count the last two years, not in the real sense of the word. They've been miserable!"

"Why, what's going on?"

"Well, there's just no closeness anymore. We seem to keep getting in each other's way. We don't seem to have anything in common. Neither one of us is happy." He used the word *seem* several times in the conversation, indicating to me that he was making a decision through his feelings, a dangerous thing to do.

I wanted to make a point. "Brian, the only grounds for divorce and remarriage is adultery. Has she been unfaithful to you?"

Brian leaned back in his chair and laughed, "Oh no, not Becky. She would never. She's a good Christian."

"What about *you*, Brian. Have *you* been faithful?"

Brian paused and looked intently at me. "I haven't been with anyone else, if that's what you mean. No, it's not that. It's just that I want to be free. I don't love her anymore."

I leaned forward and put my hand on his forearm, "Brian! You made a promise before God, for better or worse, until death. Listen, you can get counseling to help you work through the problems. I know someone who—"

Brian pulled back. "No, Randy. You're not getting what I'm saying. I don't love Becky. I don't want to be married anymore. I just want to be . . . be on my own. It's too late for counseling. I'm moving out this evening . . . just wanted you to know."

Brian was good enough to stay and let me pray with him. I asked the Lord to give him the ability to see his heart was out of fellowship with Him. I prayed for Becky and the grace she would need in the coming days. I also prayed for the protection of their two children, seven and nine years old. However, Brian's mind was firm and his heart hard. He left the restaurant resolved, displaying no second thoughts.

The next day I called Becky to check on her. She told me Brian had indeed moved out the evening before and had taken an apartment ten miles away. Two weeks later, she told me at the church building that he had almost emptied their bank account furnishing the apartment with "grand" furniture and custom-made curtains. Not long after that, he bought both a car and a motorcycle. The phrase "high, wide, and handsome" came to mind, as Brian wanted a carefree, independent, and stylish life. But his new life didn't turn out the way he thought it would.

Less than seven months later, Brian was in my office, filled with regret. Even though free from his marriage, he *still* wasn't happy. In his words, he was lonely and empty with nothing to look forward to. His days were meaningless, and his nights were unbearable. He missed Becky and the kids.

"Have you talked with her?" I asked.

"She said she *doesn't want* to talk." Brian looked away. "She's moved on."

"You mean she's found someone else?" I hadn't seen or heard of her with anyone else.

"No." Brian looked down, a sign of resignation. "She said she's learned how to get along without me."

I had suspected that might be her response. The last time I'd spoken with her I could tell she was becoming embittered. She felt rejected, embarrassed to face neighbors and friends who wanted to know where Brian was and how he was doing, showing no apparent consideration for her and the kids. And she was heavily burdened, raising two small children, maintaining the house, making repairs, looking after the animals, and running the farm. She was angry Brian had left her with a nearly empty bank account and harassing phone calls from creditors. She decided she didn't need him.

Somehow, they agreed to try. Brian sold his new furniture and motorcycle (at losses) and moved back in with Becky and the kids. However, it didn't last long, and they divorced soon after.

*****

A similar event happened about ten years later. A couple came into my office for guidance. She was a regular attender, but he only attended on special occasions. They had been married just over a year and had one child. Now, he was telling her he *never* loved her and didn't want to be married anymore. He only came to our meeting to appease her. She looked at me in such a way as to say, *You're our last-ditch effort.*

I looked at the husband and asked, "How long have you felt this way?"

"It's been several months now," he answered. I pled with him to change his mind. I offered to refer them to a professional counselor. I read scripture and prayed with them. But to no avail. He refused help, and they separated. With a baby and no income, she felt forced to return to California and live with her parents.

But just two weeks later he was back in my office crying, in fact wailing, that he wanted her back. He said now that she was gone, he realized he *did* love her after all and was so lonely he couldn't stand it. He couldn't live without her and wanted her to come back.

From my office we called her parents' home in California to ask her if she would return. "No," she said, "he's too unpredictable. We're better off here. Thank you, Randy, for trying." She hung up.

Her husband just threw his arms on the table and rested his head on them. He was sobbing. I tried to encourage him not to give up, to keep trying. I encouraged him to live for Christ and draw on strength from the fellowship of the church, but after he left my office, I never saw him again.

The next week his wife called me from California to check on her husband.

"I haven't seen or heard from him since that night," I said.

"Neither have I."

*****

"Randy, this is Paul. I'm calling from a church in Georgia to get a reference on Greg Conley."

I didn't know the minister and answered quickly. "I'm sorry, I won't give a reference for Greg." I answered quickly because I had already determined how I'd respond if asked for a reference regarding Greg. In fact, I was surprised that Greg would even name me as a reference.

Paul hesitated. I'm sure he was thinking, *That refusal in itself is a bad reference.*

"He caused a problem there, didn't he?"

"Yes."

"I knew it," Paul said. Then he sighed. "We've already hired him, but it looks like it was a mistake! He didn't list you as a reference, but there was a gap in his history and I tracked it down. I learned he was there with you for a while."

"That's true."

Another pause. "Well, I should have called you before we hired him. His stats (college grades, honors received, internship) were impressive. His college professors and intern supervisor gave him glowing reports, and he gave a great interview. In fact, we were so impressed we hired him on the spot. He's in trouble here too."

Greg showed more promise for the Lord's service than anyone I have known. He graduated with honors from Bible college, spent a year's internship at a larger church, and was then ready to start youth ministry with our teens. He was still unmarried and had lots of time and availability to conduct a dynamic youth program. As we had hoped, under his leadership, the youth ministry grew rapidly.

He quickly built strategic relationships among youth and adults to recruit for his program. In terms of organization and recruitment, he *seemed* to be supernaturally gifted by the Holy Spirit. However, in spite of his dynamic personality, honors received in school, and recommendations from superiors, Greg had a hidden weakness apparently no one knew about. Several months after he arrived, strange things started happening.

It began one Saturday night as Sandi and I waited up for our son to return from a late-night school event. Our door was open, and the porch light was on. At midnight, our doorbell rang. A young woman I judged to be in her twenties stood on our porch smiling. I opened the door, and she said, "Greg?" Greg lived alone near the church building.

I was somewhat shocked and spoke before thinking it through. I automatically responded, "No." She apologized, went to her car, checked the address then left and drove over into Greg's driveway. I stepped out on the porch and waited to see what would happen next. About two minutes later I saw her car pull out of Greg's drive and speed down the road.

The next morning, I asked Greg about it. He simply said, "She had the wrong address."

One Saturday about a month later, I was alone in the church office preparing for worship the next day when the phone rang. I answered, and a woman's voice spoke. "I want to talk to Greg," she demanded.

"I'm sorry, Greg's not here. Can I take a message?"

"Are you the main preacher?"

"I'm the senior minister. How can I help you?"

"Your youth minister is a thief! He stole over a hundred dollars from me, and I want it back."

Stunned, I tried to get more information. "What do you mean? How did he steal from you?"

"We were at a hotel last night and he took money from my wallet while I was in the shower!" She was so angry she was huffing into the phone.

"What?! Are you sure you've got the right Greg?"

"I'm positive!" She was annoyed at the question. "I can tell you where he lives and what kind of car he drives." She did.

"If you don't believe me you can call the hotel." She gave me the name and location of the hotel.

I promised her I would look into it. I offered to call her back as soon as I did, but she refused to give me her name and number. (It was a landline, and we didn't have caller ID then.) It's not easy to believe an anonymous accusation, but this along with the midnight visitor was too much to *dis*believe.

As soon as we hung up, I looked up the hotel's number to confirm the number and address. They were the same. I called, and a male clerk answered. I asked him, "Do you have a Greg Conley registered there?"

"No sir. He checked out early this morning." It was a short answer, and the tone of his voice indicated disgust.

"Okay, thank you. Oh, by the way, can you tell me *what time* he checked out?"

"Yes sir. It was one o'clock this morning."

"Okay. Thanks." I hung up the phone.

What on earth? I flopped down in my chair and tried to put the pieces of this puzzle together. No matter how I arranged them, it wasn't a good picture.

I informed the board of elders, who were shocked beyond belief. They had been pleased to see a rapid growth among the teen youth group and couldn't believe a young man as capable as Greg could do such things. Anyway, we met with Greg and asked him to explain the call.

Greg denied it all. Despite the hotel clerk's confirming his stay, Greg insisted he was not at the hotel and he did not steal money from anyone. Someone was illegally using his name, he said. The elders spoke firmly to him and cautioned him to be careful, saying they would be alert to anything inappropriate. However, they still couldn't rationalize this report with Greg's personality and success in the youth group.

For the next few weeks, more strange things were happening. More phone calls demanding Greg "make things right." He insisted these must be crazy people trying to scam him. One morning I pulled into the office wing parking lot and noticed Greg's car had been vandalized. Paint had been thrown on it, and someone had painted in large letters the word *SINNER* on both sides of his vehicle. Greg said he didn't know who they were but that he suspected a couple of boys whom he had forbidden to approach a girl in the youth group they were angry at. In all of these defenses, he presented himself as very sincere.

Greg was eventually exposed later in the summer months. It happened when he made arrangements to take the youth group to a national youth conference. Our church policy stated that the student intern would stay behind to conduct the youth program in Greg's absence. Greg knew the policy, understood it, and agreed to it when he was hired.

Our youth intern that summer was a rising senior and a great guy all around. During his internship with us, he stayed with Greg in the youth parsonage. Mike admired Greg's leadership too.

Midsummer, Greg approached me and said he'd like to take Mike on the conference trip too. I said, "No, Mike stays to lead the youth program while you're away."

On the Sunday morning when the youth were scheduled to depart for the conference, Mike showed up at the building with his suitcase. "Where are *you* going?" I asked.

Mike gave me a puzzled look. "I'm going to the conference."

"No, Mike, you're supposed to stay and service the youth program while Greg's gone."

"Well, that's what I thought, but Greg said he wanted me to go." I felt sorry for Mike. He was caught in the middle of a difficult situation.

"Wait here. I'll be right back," I said.

I asked the chairman of the elders to accompany me, he tapped another elder, and the three of us went to Greg. Greg told us he had already arranged for one of the parents to substitute for Mike. He thought it would be good for Mike to go and was sure everything would be all right. Our chairman corrected Greg and then explained to Mike he would not be going but was expected to work the youth program that week. Mike was good with that.

It soon became clear why Greg insisted on taking Mike. That night, a young woman showed up at the youth parsonage insisting her money be returned. She didn't recognize Mike and wanted to know where Greg was. When she learned that Greg was out of town, she told Mike everything. The next morning, Mike came to me, and together we met with the board of elders, who demanded Greg's resignation.

*****

9:30 p.m. Monday evening. The phone rings.

"Randy, this is Eric Thompson."

"Hello, Eric. How are you?"

"Hey, listen, Kristin and I are having a problem. Can you come over right now?"

Right now had a sense of urgency to it, alerting me there was trouble. "Sure. I'm on my way."

Within twenty minutes I was standing at the door of their apartment. Eric opened the door. "Randy. Thanks for coming."

He opened the door wider, and I walked in. Kristin was there sitting on the couch in the living room. I greeted her, and she replied with a restrained smile and a soft "Hi, Randy." I could see her eyes were red and swollen. She was nervous, constantly looking down at her hand, turning it over and looking at the palm, and then returning to the other side.

Eric walked up beside me and said, "Randy, Kristin has something to tell you."

I looked at Kristin. Her eyes were welling up with tears.

She said, "Eric wants me to tell you that Scott Rastor and I have been having an affair."

You could have knocked me down with a feather. Scott was our youth minister. I wasn't sure I'd heard correctly. "You and Scott . . . ?"

"Yes."

Eric stood beside me with his hands on his hips, glaring at Kristin. Then he told me that for the past month he had hired a detective to follow Kristin. There was no doubt. And there was no denial from her.

I sat on the couch next to her, looked at Eric, still standing there over us, then looked Kristin. "What happened?" I realized that was a stupid question. "I mean, *how* did it happen?"

Eric spoke up before Kristin could respond. "Randy, Kristin has always been attracted to the athletic type. As you know, Scott is a sports jock, big in baseball and softball.

I turned to Kristin again. "Kristin?"

Kristin raised her hands, palms up, and shrugged shoulders. "Who knows how these things start? We just spent a lot of time together in church activities . . . and one thing led to another." She said they had become good friends at first, sharing their problems about home and their dissatisfaction with their spouses. Kristin told Scott her marriage was unhappy, then Scott said his was too. She looked at me and stretched out her left palm. "And here *you* are."

Apparently, I was an act of retribution Eric was leveling at Kristin that evening. ("You're gonna face the preacher!")

"Randy, you are the last person in the world I wanted to hurt or disappoint," Kristin said.

As I sat there looking into her tearful eyes, I felt some sympathy for her. I looked at Eric, who stood solidly above us. I tried to make sense of it all. *How could this happen on my watch with a staff member? Why didn't I see it or notice something? Why? Why would Scott let this happen? How did this go on without my knowing?*

Looking back, I realized there had been signals that I didn't catch on to. Kristin spent an unusual amount of volunteer time working with the youth program. She was constantly coming to the building to meet with Scott and discuss programs. I just assumed she had taken an interest in her son's participation at church.

On another occasion, our sons had returned from teen youth camp with a video of a worship service. In that video, Scott and Kristin were sitting together during a song service. Their actions drew my attention from the teen worship to them. I felt then they were too familiar with each other, but I passed it off as a couple of casual friends relaxing during an upbeat week.

I looked up at Eric. "What now?"

"Well, obviously Kristin has broken the marriage promise we made to each other. This has been going on for at least two months. I plan to file for divorce," Eric said in the firmest voice he could muster.

I was still in shock. I had never suspected such a thing as this and walked into it blind . . . and dumb. At this point, I was unprepared and didn't know what to do but show them scriptures about marriage, faithfulness, divorce . . . and forgiveness. I asked if I could pray with them. Kristin listened submissively while Eric began to grow impatient. After about an hour, I left assuring them I would continue to pray for them.

It was nearly midnight. I went immediately to the church office and called Scott asking him to meet with me. He lived nearby and walked in promptly.

I didn't beat around the bush. "Scott, I've just come from Eric and Kristin's apartment."

"I know, Kristin called me." Scott was polite and gentle in his demeanor. There was no stubborn defiance insisting he was justified. No casting blame at his wife or anyone else. Then he added, "What do you want me to do?"

Well, I hadn't thought about that yet. Immediately I thought his effectiveness would be undermined by the affair, and it occurred to me that many parents would have trouble entrusting their children to him. I said, "I think you should submit your resignation."

Without hesitation he said, "Okay. Can I have a sheet of paper?" I handed him one, and he bent over my desk, wrote the resignation, and handed it to me.

"Scott," I said, "I'm still shell-shocked. But I think we need to pray."

"Yes."

We stood there in my office praying. I had hoped Scott would demonstrate repentance and seek forgiveness from the Lord, but he didn't, not in my presence anyway. I did the praying because Scott told me he didn't feel comfortable praying at the moment. As he walked out, I watched him walk across the parking lot. I wondered how his wife, Audra, was feeling at the moment. I've been told that experiencing a divorce has an impact much like the death of a spouse, in some cases maybe worse, as the two face friends and family who question and blame. First there's anger, then heartbreak and sorrow with loneliness. I wondered, would she forgive him?

What about Eric and Kristin? Eric had already declared he intended to divorce Kristin, but could he erase from his mind and heart several years of marriage. And their son—what about him? Would he go with Eric or with Kristin? Scott and Audra had no children to fight over, but Eric and Kristin had a nine-year-old.

Watching Scott walk back home, it became clear to me how much I loved both families. I determined to encourage forgiveness and reconciliation in both marriages.

The elders were brokenhearted and disappointed in the news, but they accepted Scott's resignation. The following Wednesday evening the chairman spoke to the congregation announcing Scott's departure. Scott had made many strong friendships in the church, so some were angry at me for asking Scott to resign.

After that meeting, I met with the youth group to comfort and guide as best I could. Many of their parents stood against the wall, watching their children as I talked. Most took it well. Even though they loved Scott, they knew what he did was wrong and would impair his effectiveness as a minister. However, one young man spoke up, "I don't see what the big deal is. It's just a sin like every other sin."

"You're right that adultery is a sin, and it can be forgiven. And I'll add that if these marriages are restored, God can bless them. But we need to keep in mind God set marriage apart from every other physical bond or commitment. He even compared our relationship with Christ to the love commitment between a husband and wife. When you guys marry, you're going to expect faithfulness from your spouse and your spouse will expect faithfulness from you. That is a right reserved in marriage. But that faithfulness to each other is built upon your faithfulness to God."

In my ministry, I had made a point of emphasizing that the purity and dignity of marriage must be protected. I had taught repeatedly that there should be no friendship or relationship closer than with one's spouse. Hebrews 13:4 says, "Marriage should be honored by all, and the marriage bed kept pure, for God will judge the adulterer and all the sexually immoral." I also pointed out that God seems to make a distinction between adultery and every other sin. 1 Corinthians 6:18–20 says, "Flee from sexual immorality. All other sins a person commits are outside the body, but whoever sins sexually, sins against their own body. Do you not know that your bodies are temples of the Holy Spirit, who is in you, whom you have received from God? You are not your own; you were bought at a price. Therefore honor God with your bodies."

After that, we prayed, nearly fifty of us in that room. We asked God to be with both families involved. We prayed for reconciliation of both marriages. We prayed for the state of marriage in our nation, and we prayed for the kingdom of God.

Over the next few weeks I made attempts to reach both couples and encourage forgiveness and reunion. Neither wanted to discuss the possibility. Two were angry, and all four wanted to just move on. I learned that Eric had asked for and received a transfer and left the area. I also learned that Scott and Kristin had moved in together.

A few weeks later, Scott and Kristin appeared at my office door asking if they could talk to me. I invited them in, and they came right to the point. They wanted to continue coming to this church . . . together, as a couple.

I looked at both of them trying to formulate a response. "Scott, I've spoken to you both about restoring your marriages. That's still my prayer, that you would go back to Audra and Kristin back to Eric. It may take time, but with God's grace, it can happen." I looked at Kristin. "Your child needs both mother and father together." Then I looked at Scott. "I want you to know I will do everything I can to help that reconciliation."

Scott said, "We've decided too much damage has been done to our marriages and we're going to stay together. We've repented, and we think God has already forgiven us. We just wanted to know if we'd be welcome here."

"Everyone is welcome here," I said, "but understand, I cannot accept this relationship as it is. You are both still married to someone else, and yet now you're living together. As someone who grew up in church, went to Bible college, and studied the Word, you know better. You're welcome to attend, but I cannot validate your relationship. I will not ask you to teach a class, work with youth, or hold a leadership position."

"Okay, understood," Scott said softly. They stood, and I walked them to the door. Scott extended his hand, and I shook it. Kristin wrapped her arms around me with a gentle embrace. With that, he and Kristin bid me goodbye and left.

A few weeks later I was told Scott and Kristin placed their membership with a sister congregation several miles from us. In spite of their cohabitation, they were received as members in good standing. Over a lunch meeting, I told the minister of that church we were working to restore their marriages. He said to me, "We didn't think they were going to do that, so we accepted them as they are."

After the divorces were finalized, Scott and Kristin were married, and they continued to serve in that church.

*****

I did not perform any of the marriages in this chapter; however, my heart still broke with each of them. Marriage is an institution ordained by God Himself, and I feel a responsibility to invest myself in strengthening that institution. I have conducted more than 100 weddings over the years, and gratefully, most of them are still intact. I thank God for His mercies.

What I Learned

1. I learned to seek out and appreciate the traits I love so much in my wife.

2. I learned to constantly remind myself that my actions affect my family and the kingdom of God

3. I learned from David in the Old Testament that a "moment of pleasure can lead to a lifetime of regret."

4. I learned that dedicated men and women are still vulnerable and in need of protection.

5. I learned to appreciate older and wiser Christians who were looking out for me.

6. I learned to pray every day for myself, my ministry staff, and church leaders.

7. I learned to admit my weaknesses and vulnerability to God.

8. I learned to strengthen my faith through devotional reading and prayer.

9. I learned that everyone has struggles in marriage.

10. I learned after prayer and Scripture reading to refer counselees to professionals.

11. I learned to limit the number of meetings with the opposite sex to no more than two.

12. I learned not to be overconfident.

13. I learned to think more about my weaknesses than my strengths.

14. I learned to talk to someone in a candidate's former ministry who is not listed as a referral.

15. I learned that integrity is more important than a dynamic personality.

Leadership Application

1. What factors do you feel contribute to the increase in sexual immorality in churches?

2. What conditions make a pastor vulnerable to temptation?

3. What policies and plans could you construct to help avoid infidelity . . .

   a. of pastors?

   b. of the congregational members?

4. How would you communicate the termination of a staff member to the congregation?

   a. When, at what point, would you reveal the investigation in impropriety? In the beginning or at the conclusion?

   b. What are your reasons?

5. References given on a resume are generally chosen by the candidate. How would you supplement your investigation of a resume?

6. In your view, why do people become disillusioned in marriage?

   a. What can the church do to help alleviate that disillusionment?

   b. What steps can churches take to strengthen marriages?

7. What responsibility do church members have toward the forsaken spouse?

8. What are the common characteristics of abuse?

   a. Of a child?

   b. Of a spouse?

9. Call three churches and ask the minister what steps are in place to identify abuse. Ask what steps are in place to report abuse.

10. Should a pastor continue preaching after an *allegation* of abuse?

11. Should a pastor who has committed adultery or abuse be allowed to continue a pulpit ministry? If so, at what point should he resume preaching?

12. What steps has your church established to investigate allegations?

13. Should pastors be held to a higher standard? Why or why not?

The Two Most Influential Men in My Life

8

MY FATHER: Ralph Childress

Bent over and without a hat, he walked alongside the road in pouring rain. With his left hand he clutched the lapels of his coat to keep his shirt dry. Dressed in an old ragged suit coat and tweed pants with worn shoes, he was short, bald, and frumpy. The expression on his face was forbidding, as if he was always embittered about something. There was a kind of mystery about him; although he had lived in our small town all his life, no one really knew him.

We saw him often because he walked by my elementary school every day at the same time, always at recess. We never knew where he came from or where he was going. Sixth grade boys would run to the four-foot chain link fence, lean over the top rail, and call out to him. We only knew him as "Hoover," and we weren't sure if that was his first name or his last name.

"HEY, HOOVER! WHATCHA DOIN', MAN? GOING TO SEE YOUR GIRLFRIEND?" They would all laugh out loud. Hoover picked up his pace because he knew what was coming next. Kids began to pick up sticks and gravel, never stones, even though there was always that possibility. Never able to actually reach him, they would throw things at him just to taunt him. He wouldn't even turn to look at them, he would walk briskly and throw his right arm out as if pushing them away, even though they were on the other side of the road and behind a fence.

I never joined in those taunts, but many of those boys were my friends. I would see them every day as we divided up into teams to play ball. Like any other boy, I wanted to be one of the first chosen. It didn't necessarily mean I was skilled athletically, but to me, it indicated whether or not they liked me. While I didn't approve of what they were doing to Hoover, I still wanted to be accepted by them.

When I reached junior high, I stayed after school for football practice and usually either caught a ride home with someone or hitchhiked. Those days, in a small community, hitchhiking was legal and fairly safe. As a hitchhiker, I stood on the side of the road with my thumb extended hoping someone who knew me would pick me up and take me home, or at least part of the way.

One afternoon, it was raining hard and my father decided he didn't want me along the road in a storm, so he was there waiting for me as soon as I walked out of the locker room. Our house was about eight miles from the school, so I was relieved I didn't have to walk in the rain.

Just minutes after we left the school building, we saw Hoover walking on the side of the road, soaking wet. Dad pulled off the road in front of him and called out, "HOOVER, COME ON! WE'LL TAKE YOU HOME!" *I can't believe it! Dad's picking Hoover up! What if my friends see us? I'll get ribbed about it tomorrow! That's it! I'm toast!*

Hoover ran to the car, slid in the back seat, and closed the door behind him. Dad then pulled back onto the road. "Hoover, it's a nasty day out. You'll get soaked."

Hoover slouched and grunted, "Yeah," then turned and stared out his side window.

Dad continued talking with Hoover as if they were longtime friends. Every now and then he'd ask a yes or no question and Hoover would respond with "yeah" or "naw," nothing else. His vocabulary seemed to be made up of only two words. I didn't know Hoover and didn't know anything to talk to him about, so I just kept quiet and never even looked at him. However, it was hard to ignore the odor that came from a wet body covered with sweat that probably hadn't been bathed in months. I wanted to roll my window down, but the wind was pelting the rain on my side of the car, so I left it up. The car reeked with Hoover's body odor.

Grundy was a small town. Everybody knew everybody else so well we recognized people in the vehicles they drove. They knew each other's business and often talked about it. As we drove on, we passed vehicles that I knew belonged to my friends' parents. Afraid they would see me, I started to slink down in my seat. *We're almost* home, I thought. Then Dad drove past the road leading to our house. I turned to look at him thinking he had missed our turn, and Dad gave me a look that communicated, *Don't you dare say a word!*

"Hoover, we're going to take you home. It's too bad out to walk it," he said to our passenger.

"Yeah."

So, we went fifteen minutes out of our way, up a hollow by way of a muddy, dirt road to drop Hoover off at his shack. When the car stopped, Hoover got out and shut the door behind him without saying a word of thanks.

After we pulled off the dirt road onto the main highway, Dad pulled the car over to the curb and turned toward me. "Randy, I've never been so ashamed of you as I am now. Are you too good to show kindness to people?"

I admit I didn't have an answer for that one, so I kept quiet.

"Hoover doesn't have all the advantages that you've had. You saw it, he didn't grow up in as nice a home as you did. He doesn't have the education you've had. And he doesn't have the health you have. Hoover is sick and may not have many more years."

I think I sheepishly started slinking in my seat again. He still wasn't done yet.

"Do you think you earned those things? They were *given* to you! *Given*! People don't *give* things to Hoover; they *take* things from him. They take his pride. They take his peace. How do you think *you'd* do if it had been you who was born there, you that people avoid and ridicule?" He paused. "Answer me!"

"I would be miserable."

"Yes, you'd be miserable. How about feeling some of that right now?"

I did. Eighth grade boys don't cry the way they did when they were children, and neither did I, but I cried nonetheless—not bawling like a first grader, but my eyes filled with tears. I was shamefaced that day and humbled for days afterward. From that day on I saw Hoover from a different perspective, through my father's eyes that gave him respect and consideration. After that day, I still wanted to be among the first chosen for a pickup game, but I no longer cared if my friends saw me speak kindly to Hoover. I never wanted my father, nor my heavenly Father, to be ashamed of me again.

*****

I wish you knew my father. You would have liked him. He had a way with people and was very popular in our small town. In fact, *he's the reason I went into ministry*. However, my earliest memory of my father is not a good one.

I must have been just three or four years old the day Mom drove up to my grandparents' house. She turned and looked at me in the back seat and said she was going into grandpa's house for a moment but would return. "Stay where you are," she said, "I'll be right back." I didn't understand why, but Mom was crying. I had never seen adults cry before, and it scared me.

The whole day was confusing to me. Mom and Dad had argued earlier, and that also scared me, but now they were calm. It was also unusual that Mom had driven while Dad sat in the passenger seat, not speaking the whole trip. I watched her exit the car, walk around to Dad's side and help him out. She sidled up next to him, put her arm around his waist, and then led him into his parent's home. I waited for them.

After a few minutes, Mom returned to the car alone, holding a tissue to her nose. She was still crying. She slid in behind the steering wheel and started the car. "Mom, don't forget Dad," I said.

She adjusted the rearview mirror to look at me and said, "Honey, Daddy's not feeling well, Grandma knows how to help him." All I could see were her eyes in the mirror, red and swollen.

Some years later, I put it all together. My father had been drunk. She couldn't handle him, so she brought him to his parents' house to sober up.

That story is replayed over and over again today in America, as thousands of homes are struggling with alcoholism, drug addiction, domestic abuse, and divorce. Having been in the ministry over forty-seven years, I have tried to minister to couples going through divorce caused by unfaithfulness, sometimes in the form of adultery, other times negligence. Broken-hearted parents, young people who feel rejected, worthless, and unloved, their lives spiraling downward. I want you to know that Jesus Christ can make a difference in your life, your marriage, and your home. If you will honestly turn to him, you'll begin reordering your priorities in life. You can't do it by yourself. The proof is in the number of attempts that have failed. You need to surrender to Jesus.

Do you think that statement is simplistic? Maybe you're thinking to yourself, *It won't work. I've tried everything.* But you haven't tried everything until you've brought yourself under the influence of Christ. I know, because I've seen it again and again.

That's why I wish you knew my father. My earliest memory of him is of my crying mother, but praise God, Dad left me with many more memories, *better* memories. He invited Christ into his life and was changed. He became a new creature in Christ.

How did it happen? The only thing I know is that one Sunday morning they sent their eight-year-old son (me) off on the church bus that stopped by our house. Bus ministry was big in those days. Mom told me later that as the bus drove off, Dad watched from the window. He turned to her and said, "Alice, it's not right that we *send* Randy to church. Next week, we'll *take* him."

The next Sunday, my parents dressed up, loaded me in the car, and attended church with me. Once they started attending, they didn't miss a service unless they were sick or out of town. Our minister, Preacher Greenleaf, preached strong, powerful sermons, and Dad listened to every one of them. After several weeks, he heard a sermon that the Holy Spirit drove into his heart and he walked forward responding to the invitation.

He made a commitment to Christ that day and was baptized at the Grundy Church of Christ. From then on, he was faithful, attending worship and participating in the church's ministry. He even started taking Bible courses at the local Bible institute. He seemed to have a genuine hunger for the Word of God. Week after week he was becoming more of a *new man* and *less of what he was*. He *wanted* this change in his life and was willing to stretch himself for it. I remember the first time the preacher called on him to pray publicly. I was standing next to him in a morning worship service when Preacher Greenleaf spoke his name and asked him to close the service out in prayer. He leaned forward and took hold of the pew in front of him with both hands. I could feel that pew shake as he trembled, yet he prayed. Dad overcame his fear of speaking publicly, raised his voice, and prayed God's blessings upon us all.

Eventually Dad was asked to teach a Sunday school class. With no more than an eighth grade education, he sat at his desk for hours at a time studying commentaries, writing his manuscript out by hand, each lesson he wrote about twenty pages, practicing it out loud while mom and I watched television in another room. If he finished his lesson early, he started on the next one. Before long he maintained a stack of lessons that were over a foot high on his desk. He was growing in Bible knowledge, and he was deepening in his prayer life. At nights, from my bedroom, I could hear him praying for me, for the church, and for the sick as he and mom knelt by their bedside. It does something to your spirit to hear your parents pray for you every night. When I was away at college, I remembered my parent's prayers for me. As a junior high schooler, I would lie in bed at night waiting to drift off to sleep when I would hear Dad's voice from across the hall praying. He always included me in his prayers.

Dad was asked to be a deacon, and he regularly attended those board meetings, helped serve the Lord's Supper in worship services, and delivered communion to shut-ins, spending time with them and asking them if they needed anything. He served as treasurer of the church for three years, keeping the church's financial books. He wrote checks and paid the church bills while at the same time preparing a Sunday school lesson, checking on his class members, serving as a deacon, *and* maintaining a full-time job as a car salesman.

Then, he was asked to serve as an elder. For Dad, this was the highest honor a man could have. He was humbled and grateful that the preacher and the church board had confidence in him. He never missed a board meeting unless he was too ill to attend. If we went out of town, he made sure we returned in time for him to attend.

Finally, Dad was asked to serve as chairman of the board of elders. He held that position for a few years until the Lord laid a different ministry on his heart. He wanted to preach the Word!

Early on in my life, Dad was a barber. Then he took a part-time job selling used cars with the dealership next to the barber shop. He saved his money and started his own used car business. Leasing a small piece of land on the main road leading into Grundy, he began with three used cars, then there were seven, then twelve, and on and on until he had expanded the property and maintained a lot with over thirty used cars and even some campers. He treated people right, warrantying the cars he sold, and soon had a reputation as a fair and honest businessman. I helped him by washing and waxing cars and changing tags when they sold.

My senior year in high school, he left the car business and opened a shoe store—first one, then another in a neighboring town and a third even further away. The shoe business flourished.

He had come a long way from that drunken man, and if you asked him how that change took place, he'd tell you in two words: "Jesus Christ." He always felt God blessed him so he could bless the work of the church, God's kingdom on earth. I remember standing with him in the church foyer one Sunday when a visiting missionary from Africa, Dr. Dennis Pruett, spoke at our church. I watched as he subtly slipped a check in Dr. Pruett's hand. "Oh no, Ralph," Dr. Pruett said, "you don't have to do this. The church has already taken care of my expenses."

"Yes, I do, Dennis. God has already blessed me for giving it." Dad directly influenced hundreds, and indirectly through his support, he influenced thousands.

He was offered and he accepted the position of trustee at Kentucky Christian College, and it was during this time smaller, area-wide churches started calling him to preach. He discovered preaching the Word was his greatest joy.

The Eighties hit Grundy hard. The recession devastated the coal industry, which employed most workers in the mountainous area, and they closed their mines. Thousands of people in our small town were out of work. With an unemployment rate of over 15%, no one was spending money because there was no money to spend. The population of the area declined along with the economy as young couples moved away to find work elsewhere, and so the shoe business suffered. In that trying time, Dad saw an opportunity to do what he felt God was calling him to do. He closed his three stores, retired, and started helping churches in the area.

Now he was free to serve the Lord as he wanted. He would go up in the hollows to small congregations of thirty or forty people that had no preachers to fill the pulpit, teaching and preaching the gospel of Christ. His only income was Social Security, and when churches *did* pay him he refused to keep it. Instead, he bought window air conditioners for the elderly in those churches who couldn't afford them. He used the money they paid him to repair leaking roofs and perform other maintenance repairs for elderly members.

Dad's funeral was one of the largest attended funerals ever held in Grundy, VA. I wish you knew him. You would have liked him. My earliest memory of my father was not a good one, but that memory has been overshadowed by so many other memories, *good* memories left to me. He became a loving husband, loving father, an important member of the community, a leader in the church, and a minister in the kingdom of God. That kind of transformation can only be accomplished by the Lord. When I hear 2 Corinthians 5:17—"Therefore, if anyone is in Christ, the new creation has come: The old has gone, the new is here!"—I automatically remember the change Christ worked in Dad's life.

Although he didn't smoke or work in a coal mine, later in his life, Dad developed a lung condition known as bronchiectasis. Doctors couldn't control the fungus that jumped from one part of his lung to the other. Little by little pieces of his lungs were excised, but in just a few years the fungus unrelentingly corroded them. Before he passed, he was admitted to the University of Virginia Medical Center. Mom and I walked in to the ICU to visit him, even though he was sedated and didn't know we were there. We stood beside him, held his hand, and prayed when a team of doctors interrupted us to examine him. Mom walked out immediately, but I lingered to find out what I could from the doctors. Before leaving, I turned to the lead doctor and said, "Take care of him. He's the best man I've ever known."

A few months later, the best man I've ever known passed into glory to live forever with the Savior he served so faithfully. He was sixty-eight years old, and the last forty years of his life impacted hundreds of lives, but no one was influenced more than I. I have no doubt about Dad's eternal destination; it's all wrapped up in Jesus.

You see, that's why I entered the ministry. If Jesus Christ can change a man from a drunkard separated from his family into the best man his son has ever known, *I've got to tell people about Jesus.*

*****

MY PREACHER: Clarence Greenleaf

Preacher Clarence Greenleaf and his wife Louise became Mom and Dad's best friends. They visited each other, went to dinner with each other, and even took vacation trips together. That's how I knew the Greenleafs. It may also be the reason Preacher Greenleaf approached me to fill the youth minister's position at the Grundy church.

In college, I spent four years majoring in biology with the intention of going to medical school. Our family was acquainted with the head of the department of hematology at UVA, and we thought he might have pull with the admission department.

However, one summer Preacher Greenleaf contacted me and asked if I would take the position as youth minister. I thought I would enjoy playing sports and games with the kids, so I told him that or the summer I would be the director but not the youth minister. I soon discovered my heart was in ministry and Mom and Dad encouraged me to follow my heart.

I spent over five years working under Preacher Greenleaf's direction. He used every opportunity to teach both Scripture and ministry. Whenever we travelled, I drove the car while he taught. I still remember him slapping the dash. "Acts 2, Randy. *This* is what was spoken by the prophet Joel," he said, teaching me church doctrine. I took classes under him at the Bible institute and grew in both knowledge and faith.

He was a unique man who both loved sports and loved to read. It was an unusual combination, but you never saw him without a book and a pencil. He never used a pen; it was always a pencil. He wrote his letters in pencil. He wrote his sermons in pencil. He made notes in pencil. Years later, I looked at some of his sermon notes but the lead markings had all but faded away. *What a tragedy,* I thought, *over seventy years of experience gone!* He's the reason I wanted to write this book. My wife asked me what the purpose of this book would be. "To leave something behind," I said.

Preacher Clarence Greenleaf was a popular speaker in demand for revivals and conventions across the country. Three years I drove him to the Kiamichi Men's Clinic in the mountains of Oklahoma. For several years he had been one of the main speakers, and now they had honored him by placing him on the "watchdog session" annually. The watchdog session featured speakers whose job was to make sure the clinic was following its mission of promoting Christ and His kingdom.

One year in particular comes to my mind. It was the early Eighties. The last three decades had been a time of anxiety, as a fear of communism had spread across the nation. It was addressed in politics, communities, and churches as well as the Kiamichi Men's Clinic. This particular year, more than 10,000 men gathered under a metal canopy as popular radio speaker Paul Harvey addressed the congregation on the first night. Harvey was outstanding! As he walked off the stage, he received a rousing applause.

The following day, speaker after speaker stood on the platform and railed against communism. Finally, during the afternoon watchdog session, Preacher Greenleaf stood and began. "Brothers, I hate communism . . ." A chorus of "amens" waved across the audience. Then he slapped the pulpit, hard. It sounded as if a cannon had been fired nearby. Men startled by the sudden noise jumped, and if they weren't paying attention before, they were now. Preacher Greenleaf said, "I DO! I hate communism. BUT I HATE SIN MORE!" The men stood and clapped, prompting him, "Preach it, brother! Tell it, Greenleaf!" He launched into a powerful sermon that preachers and churches ought to be railing against sin. "We're not here to fight communism," he proclaimed. "We're here to preach Christ and Him crucified. We're here to fight the devil and sin! The problem breaking up homes and marriage, the problem destroying lives is not communism, but sin! The devil has distracted us!" he said. "We're so busy fighting political battles we've forgotten what the real war is about. We've forgotten WHO the real enemy is. Our battle is not against flesh and blood, but against principalities and powers, against spiritual wickedness in high places!"

Thousands of men were rallying the cry. When Greenleaf stepped off the platform, there was a standing ovation and someone started singing "Victory in Jesus." It sent chills down my spine to hear thousands of male voices singing praise.

The men around me were nodding their heads in approval. "That Greenleaf! He's a powerful speaker, and he's right! We need more of that kind of preaching," they said. And it occurred to me that I had been hearing that kind of preaching for years. *Yep! That's my preacher!*

Clarence Greenleaf was bold. When the county opened its first ABC store (state-run alcoholic beverage store), he took a portable public address system in his car and parked on the side of the road nearby, and when people went in to buy alcohol, he would call out to them. "Hey! The Bible says don't look upon the wine when it's red!" Or "Hey! Shame on you! Your children need shoes! Your wife needs a new dress!"

People became angry with him, but no one could *stay* angry with him because he loved them all. No other preacher in the county had preached more funerals or conducted more weddings than he.

One wedding he performed for a couple stands out in my mind. A sweet mountain girl was marrying a rough, profane man. Preacher knew both families, and he didn't want her to marry him, but they would have gone to the justice of the peace and Greenleaf would have nothing invested in their marriage. So he decided to perform the small wedding. After he pronounced them man and wife, he took the young man by the arm, pulled him over to the side out of sight of most people, put his fist up in the man's face, and said, "If you ever hit her, this is what you're gonna get!" (I found out later he was a boxer while in high school, in Charleston, West Virginia.)

He preached funerals for mountain folk who had no resources to pay him. Once, he preached a funeral and the two of us helped the funeral director and his assistant, four people in all, carry the heavy casket nearly a quarter of a mile up an inaccessible snow-covered dirt road to a small family graveyard in the mountains. I think I was in my mid-twenties, but that casket was heavy. It wasn't easy for either of us. Not once, however, did he say, "They should have taken care of this." It was always, "I'm so glad we could do something to help." He laughed when people laughed, and he wept when people wept. He could hobnob with the rich and the poor. He was accepted and loved by both.

He was always upbeat. At odd times he'd just break out in a praise song. When dealing with tragedy, he would reach both hands around someone's neck, lock his fingers, pull their forehead to touch his, and pray with them. As he listened to them he would say, "Mercy! Mercy, mercy, mercy."

He had a wonderful sense of humor. Even children and teenagers enjoyed being with him. He was always clowning around, so relaxed around people, never trying to put on airs. He never insisted on respect; he earned it.

One summer, I conducted a week-long creation seminar for high schoolers. I invited Dr. John Morris from the Institute of Creation Research to be our guest. During one of the day sessions, I spoke to a gathering of teens about how ridiculous it was to think we had descended from apes. At that, they started laughing and pointing behind me. I turned to see Preacher Greenleaf walking across the stage knees bent with his knuckles on the floor and his chin stuck out, modeling an ape. Then he turned to the teens and scratched under his arm, pulled off an imaginary flea, and pretended to eat it. I gave up and sat down laughing with them. Then Greenleaf broke out into a song the "Singing Fireman," Eddie Jones of Richmond, Virginia, had written: "I'm no kin to the monkey, no, no, no. The monkey's no kin to me, yeah, yeah, yeah. I don't know much about your ancestors, but mine didn't swing in a tree."

These character and personality traits contributed to a dynamic ministry in the small coal mining town of Grundy, Virginia.

Clarence Greenleaf became the minister of Grundy Church of Christ just after the Great Depression. The church was a small congregation of less than forty people meeting in an old one-room white frame building with two potbelly stoves. The building caught fire one February night in 1941 and burned to the ground. As they stood there looking at the burned pulpit, chairs, and building wondering what they would do next, an elderly woman hobbled over to him, put two one-dollar bills in Preacher Greenleaf's hand, and said, "Build it back!"

That command stirred Preacher's heart. This woman reminded him of the poor widow who gave her gift of two mites (Luke 21:1–4); it was all she had. He preached his heart out: "Can God take a couple of dollars and rebuild a church? Yes! He took a couple of fish and few loaves of bread to feed 5,000 people; He can rebuild this church!"

Preacher Greenleaf went to work. He evangelized the town. He evangelized the hollows. He evangelized the coal operators. Within ten years the Grundy Church of Christ building had been constructed, remodeled, and added on to twice. They built a three-story building and established the Grundy Bible Institute for the training of preachers, elders, and Sunday School teachers. He had great expectations of all those who accepted a leadership responsibility. The front wall of the worship center had a board with twenty-one light bulbs, each bulb representing an elder. When the elder was present, he turned that light on to demonstrate how dedicated the church's leaders were. None of them ever wanted their light to be dark.

On the back wall, as you exited the worship center, was the "Light of Evangelism" lit each Sunday evening. For twenty-six years, Grundy Church of Christ had at least one person in the evening service who had never been.

Young and old, rich and poor, high and low attended and sat together in the same worship center. When I was a teenager in high school, I looked at the attendance board posted on the wall that read, *Record Attendance:*

1,265. That attendance was reached Easter Sunday in 1957, in a town with just over 5,000 people.

The Grundy church had expanded physically all it could. No more property was available to it. So, through the Bible Institute, they trained young Timothys to go out and establish new congregations. Within forty miles, twenty-three new churches had been started.[1]

*****

SPECIAL MENTION: Doctor Joshua Sutherland

Figure 2 From left to right: "Preacher" Clarence Greenleaf, Dr. Joshua Sutherland, Ralph Childress

For two years while in college, I spent my summer vacations working in the lab at Sutherland Clinic in Grundy, VA. Majoring in biology, I intended to go to medical school and thought my lab experience would help getting through the Admissions Department.

Dr. Sutherland was a "medical pioneer" in Grundy, treating people from the mountains and hollows without charge if they were unable to pay. He was considered one of the great citizens of the county. He was also an Elder in the Grundy Church of Christ and supported the ministry, Bible colleges and foreign missions.

When I decided to go into ministry rather than medicine, I dreaded telling Dr. Sutherland. He had invested two summers in my future medical career and I wondered how he would respond.

---

[1] Joseph E. O'Neal, *Preacher Greenleaf* (New York: Century of Recovery, 1990), p. 19.

He looked at me with a slight smile and said, "You know, Randy, as a doctor you can treat people and help them live good, healthy long lives."

He paused for a moment and them smiled broadly, "But as a preacher, you can lead them to eternal life!"

He encouraged my decision.

A shoe salesman gave me another good answer. When I told him I was entering full time ministry, he said. "Yeah, but you're still dealing with heels and soles (souls)."

Ralph Childress and Clarence Greenleaf were the two most influential men in my life. From my father, I learned hard work, sincerity, compassion, and devotion to the Lord. From my preacher I learned to be bold and devoted to the Word of God and the kingdom of God, the church. Now, at seventy years old, I look back and realize how blessed I have been to have these two men in my life. I wish that everyone had the influence of these two men, a father and a preacher, in their lives. For those who do not, *God help us to be* those influences in the lives of others.

Leadership Application

1. Who are the most influential people in your walk for Christ? How have they influenced you?

2. Do a search of Acts and the Epistles. Who were the people Paul mentored, and how did he influence each?

3. How is the word *new* used in the Bible (Ephesians 4:22–24; 2 Corinthians 5:7; 1 Peter 1:3)?

4. Who can you influence in ministry? What needs can you help with?

5. How would you like to be remembered? What will be your legacy?

6. What did the apostle Paul mean when he said, "Follow my example, as I follow the example of Christ" (1 Corinthians 11:1)?

7. What is the fastest growing ministry you are aware of? Why do you think it grew so quickly?

   a. What percentage of growth was due to the personality of the pastor? Explain.

   b. What percentage of growth was due to the style of music? Explain.

   c. What percentage of growth was due to the sermons? Explain.

   d. What percentage of growth was due to the programming? Explain.

8. What does it mean to have a hunger and thirst for Christ? (Matthew 5:6) How have you recognized this in your life?

9. What issues or things distract us from our calling to preach Christ? How can we bring our message back to Jesus (1 Corinthians 2:2)?

10. In 1 Corinthians 2:2, Paul writes, "For I resolved to know nothing while I was with you except Jesus Christ and him crucified." How do we make that resolution and maintain it?

11. What does it mean to be "made perfect in Jesus Christ" (Hebrews 10:13–14, 12:23)?

The Best Definitions of Leadership

Blessed are the peacemakers, for they will be called children

of God

Matthew 5:9

Peacemakers who sow in peace reap a harvest of righteousness.

James 3:18

Just a few miles from our home were several national chain eating establishments: hamburgers, Mexican, fried chicken, even a national cafeteria. Notice I use the word *were*, past tense. They're no longer there. Each one has closed. My wife and I saw it coming and feel we know the reason for each one. At the hamburger place, the manager was too familiar with the workers and had difficulty giving them direction. The other three buildings were not kept up. Their bathrooms, tables, and floors were always dirty, so families stopped dining with them.

Location was not the problem, because other restaurants have moved into those facilities and thrived over the past ten years. The issue was in management, in leadership.

Just like businesses, churches often tend to look at leadership through distorted lenses, such as the following:

The lens of popularity: choosing a leader on the basis of how much people like a person. Popularity means a potential leader is known and liked by the congregants. As the church grows, however, fewer people will be acquainted with the candidate and so they must depend on the current leaders' nominations.

The lens of the secular leadership: choosing a local business leader. It seems reasonable to think leading in a business community would make someone a good leader in the church. Many congregations appoint a successful business leader to the position of leadership thinking secular success already demonstrates leadership qualities. However, leadership in the church is radically different from leadership in the business community. In the business world, you have an employer and employees with paychecks. On the other hand, church leaders mostly work with volunteers. That's a big difference. Secular business often pushes employees for more sales, higher goals, etc. Church leaders don't push; they get out in front and lead. Congregants have confidence in their leaders' character and follow.

The lens of personality: choosing someone with a strong, authoritative nature. These are people who tend to be controlling, demanding, and dictatorial. Decisions are made on the basis of *his* preferences in music style, programs, and ministries as well as how the money is spent.

The lens of age: choosing someone because of age. Taking the word "elder" literally, they think an older man would make a better leader. However, now seventy years old, I realize the older I get, the less I like change, even though change may be necessary for the health and effectiveness of the church. To quote the Illustrated Bible Dictionary: "Growing older, however, did not necessarily mean growing wiser. Wisdom could be with the young rather than the old. Therefore elders had to be chosen carefully."[2]

How long has he been a Christian? How much experience in church membership and ministry has he had? A fifty-year-old man may have been converted at forty years of age while a forty-year-old man was converted at ten, giving the younger candidate twenty years' experience more than the older. Spiritual maturity is more important than chronological maturity.

The lens of desperation: choosing someone to fulfill a scheduled election.

Leader one: "It's time for church elections, we need to put someone up for leadership. Who can we choose?"

A long pause.

Leader two: "Let's elect Tom. He's a good man."

Leader three: "Tom is not that consistent in his attendance. We're lucky to see him once a month. He doesn't attend a small group and isn't involved in any of the ministry teams."

Leader two: "I know, but if he's a leader, he'll step up. I'm sure of it."

Leader three: "But don't you think we should wait to see if he's committed?"

Leader two: "I said he would step up, didn't I? We have to elect someone. The election is scheduled every December."

Leader one: "All in favor of Tom, say aye."

---

[2] James Orr, MA, DD, General Editor, "Entry for 'ELDER,'" *International Standard Bible Encyclopedia*, 1915, https://www.biblestudytools.com/dictionary/elder/.

Roll call vote: "Aye." "Aye." "Aye." "Aye." "Aye."

Leader one: "All those opposed, say nay."

Leader three: "Nay."

Leader one: "Motion passed. Tom is our new officer. Everyone welcome him aboard. Someone let him know . . . *if you see him.*"

This is a bad way to elect a leader.

What, then, is the right way of looking at leadership? Over the years I've heard a number of good definitions of leadership. One of the best is "Leadership is influence." I think that's a great way to think of leadership. However, recently I've noticed other important qualities in effective leaders I've known. Having worked with scores of church leaders, I've realized effective church leaders are also problem solvers, change agents, and peacemakers.

1. PROBLEM SOLVER

Leaders are problem solvers. Wherever I go, I've noticed this about effective leaders: when a problems occurs, they run *to* the problem, not away from it. I'm not saying leaders create problems—although I've certainly known some in leadership positions who have caused more problems than they've solved. What I'm saying is, when a problem becomes evident, leaders don't avoid it, hoping it will go away. Instead, they identify and resolve it using God's Word as a guide. That means they must be familiar with the Word.

I count good, effective elders among my greatest blessings as a preacher. There were times when I went to them with problems, and they readily accepted. They dealt with gossip in the church, family squabbles, and divisive personalities. They would assign teams of two to interact with the people involved and report back to the board of elders. Once, when a staff member was engaged in conflict with church members, two elders were assigned to mediate that conflict to a resolution. The elders I worked with at Kempsville acted like the shepherds they were to bring the flock back together again and maintain a spiritual demeanor in the church. From finances to building and property management to spiritual concerns, these men were faithful. I love them deeply for their commitment to the Lord and to Kempsville Christian Church.

Too many smaller churches have boards that are filled with "good ol' boys," long-standing members who have been faithful in attendance and tithing but who handle problems with avoidance, denial, and shifting of responsibility. They were elected because of long-time membership and likeability, not necessarily because of leadership traits. Problems intimidate them, especially when church friends complain. Then, suddenly life in leadership is not as gratifying or prestigious as it once was. The status quo has been interrupted, and the turmoil has made them uncomfortable. Something has to be done, though, so what do they do? They unload the problem on the preacher.

The preacher, on the other hand, has not been at the church as long as the leaders or the complainers, has not yet had enough time and opportunity to build credibility and confidence in his ministry, has less influence than the elders, and suddenly he has become "the enemy," the focus of church complaints.

I once received a phone call from a small church in North Carolina interviewing a young man who had grown up in the congregation I served. I knew him and his family well. I knew he loved the Lord and wanted to serve faithfully. I asked them, "What is it you're looking for in a preacher?"

"Randy, our church is dying. All our members, about fifty of them, are over fifty years of age. We need someone to come in and revitalize this church. I remember when we ran a hundred and fifty on Sunday mornings. We need young people! We'd love to see young families and children here. We thought if we hired a younger man he'd help draw these young people."

"So, what you've been doing in the past is not drawing young couples. Is that it?" I asked.

"That's right. We need someone to come in and help this church grow."

"You've admitted the need to do things differently. That means making some changes," I said. "Change is hard. Are you willing to support him when people complain about the changes?"

"Yes sir! We'll stand right beside him."

And true to their word, they did stand beside him . . . for about a month. After that, the young preacher and older church parted ways, and the older church continued to decline.

No wonder young preachers are leaving the ministry. According to Lifeway Facts and Trends, at least 250 pastors leave the ministry every month.[3] Pastoral Care Inc. reports only one out of every ten pastors will actually retire as a pastor.[4] Scripturally qualified and capable church leaders are essential to church health and growth.

Have you noticed what's happening across the country? New churches are popping up while older churches are dying. Why? Because it's easier to start a new church than change an old one.

2. CHANGE AGENTS

Leaders embrace the Great Commission with both arms, set goals and priorities aligned with the New Testament, develop a mission statement, and guide the church accordingly. They're "compassionate motivators." That is, they encourage congregational cooperation and growth. They understand change has to continuously happen and determine when and how the changes should be implemented. They know the building will be changed, such as by restructuring classrooms, replacing carpet and furniture, updating the children's department, or upgrading the

---

[3] Mark Dance, "Pastors Are Not Quitting in Droves," *Lifeway*, September 28, 2016, https://factsandtrends.net/2016/09/28/pastors-are-not-quitting-in-droves/.

[4] "Statistics in the Ministry," *Pastoral Care, Inc.*, accessed May 1, 2019, https://www.pastoralcareinc.com/statistics/.

technology of the youth ministry. They know style of music may change as well to effectively reach new members. Even solid preaching of the Word can be enhanced through changes in the worship center, perhaps even the addition of upgraded communication technology such as speakers, acoustic panels, microphones, video screens, etc.

Not long after I arrived at Kempsville, one of the older elders approached me privately. Putting his hand on my shoulder, he said, "Randy, if you have anything that needs to be done, any changes, you work with us (the elders) and let us carry it to the church." I understood him to mean that if I could convince them of the need for change, the elders would see to its implementation.

Over the more than thirty years I served at Kempsville, we added on to the building five times, built a new children's center and a new fellowship hall, bought three pieces of property adjacent to church property, and constructed a new worship center. Once we worked out all the details in elders' meetings, the leadership administered the changes. They publicly announced their support; whenever funds were needed, *they* went to the congregation with the appeal; *they* appointed a couple of elders to oversee each project. These men were wonderful! What a blessing they have been to me!

3. PEACEMAKERS

There's a difference between peace*keepers* and peace*makers*. Peacekeepers are willing to compromise their values in order to keep the peace. Peacemakers, on the other hand, build peace on the foundation of truth. If anything, church leaders are peacemakers.

As a child I loved watching the old Westerns. I still do as an adult. Occasionally a Western story will be about the town sheriff or a marshal referred to as the "peacekeeper." I asked Google, "What does it mean to keep the peace?" The answer came back: "refrain or prevent others from disturbing civil order."[5] In other words, there's a solid foundation for peace. "The law is the law," the sheriff would say. The foundation for the church leader is the Word of God.

One winter, I had the opportunity to attend a leadership clinic at First Baptist Church of Jacksonville, Florida, a church that held a membership of 20,000 members! First Baptist was a dynamic church known for dynamic music (at the time Southern gospel, now contemporary) and strong, dynamic preaching. Over 100 people filled the choir loft behind the preacher's platform. Technology was evident everywhere—lights, video cameras, and multiple screens. The pews in the worship center were packed.

What made this church so impressive was that it was located in the middle of downtown Jacksonville, a section of the city that was dying out. As businesses closed, the church bought the buildings and renovated them into classrooms, meeting rooms, and fellowship halls. First Baptist Jacksonville now stretches out over nine square blocks in the city. Until they bought a parking building, people were willing to park in other parts of the city and walk as much as 200 yards to the worship center. All this from a church that began in 1838 with six charter members. It has been nicknamed "the Miracle of Downtown Jacksonville."

As you can imagine, the worship service was powerful! Not just the choir singers but attendants in the pews were singing exuberantly at the tops of their voices. Everyone was positive and upbeat. Greeters stood at each of the many doors welcoming people and answering their questions. Scores of ushers were helping people find seats and asking those already seated to move over and make room. Believe it or not, everyone willingly complied! Joyfully!

Well, as you can imagine, I was both impressed and excited. I was excited with the positive attitudes of so many people and impressed with their compliance. Through the leadership seminar, I was able to see this church was highly organized and made no allowance for carelessness. If a

---

[5] "keep the peace," *Oxford English Dictionary*, accessed May 1, 2019, https://en.oxforddictionaries.com/definition/us/keep_the_peace.

church leader was not living up to his promised commitment, he would be moved to less important responsibilities and then, if no improvement, would be graciously retired from leadership.

So yes, I was impressed, *but not as impressed as I was about to be.* At one of the worship services, I was sitting next to an older lady I guessed to be in her mid-eighties. After a rousing song, the worship leader told us to stand and get acquainted with the person next to us. She turned to me and introduced herself, then asked, "Is this your first time at First Baptist?"

The smile must have been obvious on my face. "Yes! This is a beautiful church building, and it's an exciting place to be."

"Where are you from?" she asked.

"From Virginia. I'm here for the leadership clinic."

"Oh, yes," she said. "Is everything going well with the clinic?"

"It's great!" I paused. "Can I ask you a question?"

"Certainly."

"What drew you to this church? Was it the music? The choir? The preaching?"

"No," she said, "all those are wonderful, but I came for a different reason. Ten years ago, I belonged to a smaller church, about 150 members. But they fought all the time. You could feel the tension every time you walked into their building. We were forced to take sides. If you talked to one side, the other side was angry with you. I couldn't take it anymore. I've been coming here for over ten years, and I've never sensed any tension. I guess they handle all their problems in the leadership so we can worship Christ."

I guess they handle all their problems in the leadership so we can worship Christ. Leaders do what they do so we can worship Christ. That's a good description for leadership, and I've never forgotten it.

What I Learned

- I learned to carefully examine the commitment of a candidate before recommending him.

- I learned the eldership is less about popularity and personality and more about spiritual commitment and character.

- I learned leadership makes the difference in the effectiveness of ministry and outreach.

- I learned the greatest human resource available to me was my board of elders.

- I learned to trust the collective wisdom of my elders.

- I learned to appreciate the elders' willingness to face difficult challenges and give the Lord and His church priority.

- I learned to appreciate the support and encouragement I received from the eldership.

- I learned to be grateful for leaders who would get out front, set an example, and show the way.

Leadership Application

1. Read 1 Timothy 3:1–12 and Titus 1:5–9. List and rank the characteristics of leadership named, with 1 being the lowest ranking and 5 being the highest.

    a. How would you rate yourself with these qualities?

    b. Which quality gives you the most difficulty?

2. What is your understanding of "tested" in 1 Timothy 3:10? How would we do that?

3. Why do you think 1 Timothy 3:6 emphasizes "not a recent convert?" How do you think a candidate would prove himself?

4. Why do you think family management (1 Timothy 3:4–5) is important?

5. Some churches determine the number of elders based on a formula (twenty families to one elder); others opt to open eldership election each year regardless of congregational size. What are the advantages and disadvantages of each?

6. How would you like to see church leadership and ministers cooperate?

7. Most churches honor a minister with an annual Pastor Appreciation Day. How should a church honor it's other leaders (1 Timothy 5:17)?

8. Does your church sponsor a leadership training program? What does it consist of?

Every Christian Should Visit the Holy Land Every Minister MUST Visit the Holy Land

"Randy, you can't tell from these photos." Those words revealed Dad's disappointment. He and Mom had two days earlier returned from a weeklong vacation to the Grand Canyon. He picked up another photo, inspected it, and let it drop to the table. "These pictures don't do it justice. You can't see the magnitude, scope, and depth of these canyons. They're fantastic!"

I knew he was right. While I'd never visited the Grand Canyon, I had seen it while on a flight to California. The pilot announced over the PA, "Ladies and Gentlemen, we are currently passing over the Grand Canyon. We're going to make an arc around the canyon so you can see it from your cabin window." The plane banked left in the turn, and I was almost looking straight down at the canyon. It was incredibly immense! I didn't have the same perspective my father had at ground level, but I understood his frustration in trying to describe it.

A tour of the Holy Land is somewhat like that. We read about the sites, see pictures, and hear Sunday school lessons and sermons about places in the Bible. However, there's a world of difference between reading about something and personally experiencing it. Like the Grand Canyon, it is impossible to grasp in a photo. You must experience it! Some vacations last for months, maybe even a year, but a trip to the Holy Land will change your life!

My wife and I have made four trips to the Holy Land, each one more exciting, more fulfilling, and more gratifying than the ones before it. How do you explain that?

On our first trip we began with Roman Caesarea (Caesarea Maritime), a beautiful site on the coast of the Mediterranean Sea. Caesarea was an elegant sea fortress built by King Herod the Great to honor Caesar Augustus. We walked through the ruins listening as our guide, Yossi, described the beautiful architecture and artwork used in construction. There was a Roman theatre as well as a hippodrome to accommodate horse and chariot races. It was colossal. As we stood on a platform and looked out at a harbor that stretched over forty acres to accommodate up to 300 ships, Yossi described the apostle Paul's trial before Festus. He read from Acts 25:8–12:

> Then Paul made his defense: "I have done nothing wrong against the Jewish law or against the temple or against Caesar."
> Festus, wishing to do the Jews a favor, said to Paul, "Are you willing to go up to Jerusalem and stand trial before me there on these charges?"
> Paul answered: "I am now standing before Caesar's court, where I ought to be tried. I have not done any wrong to the Jews, as you yourself know very well. If, however, I am guilty of doing anything deserving death, I do not refuse to die. But if the charges brought against me by these Jews are not true, no one has the right to hand me over to them. I appeal to Caesar!"

At this point, Yossi reached out, grabbed my coat sleeve, and pulled me toward him. He whipped me around until I was facing the Mediterranean and continued the Scripture passage:

After Festus had conferred with his council, he declared:

Yossi stopped again, pointed to the ground, and said, "Paul stood here!" Then he finished the scripture:

"You have appealed to Caesar. To Caesar you will go!"

He rested his right arm on my right shoulder and pointed westward across the Mediterranean toward Italy. I looked out across the beautiful blue sea in the direction he pointed, and all of a sudden, realization hit me! *I AM STANDING IN THE VERY PLACE IT HAPPENED! All these years I have read this passage of Scripture, and I'm standing here.* I couldn't believe it, yet it was true.

Maybe you laugh. How can you know if you were standing in the same place Paul stood? With his left hand Yossi pointed to a rock by his left foot and with his other hand to another rock by his right foot. "Whether it was this rock or that rock," he said, "it was *this place!*"

I've always known the Bible's description of Paul's trial was factual, but that passage of Scripture has never been so *real* to me as it was at that moment. Now when I preach from Acts 25, I see Caesarea in my mind; I'm familiar with it. Like describing a town from a previous trip, remembering where the courthouse, a restaurant, or a church building was, seeing it in your mind's eye, you've been there and you know the place.

THE JOURNEY

"Well, they didn't find my revolver."

Rhoda was a spry eighty-year-old woman making the trip to Israel with us. She had been randomly selected by airport security in Norfolk, Virginia to be searched. She came out from behind a curtain, trying to juggle her coat, her purse, and her carry-on while clamping her boarding pass between her teeth. Never having traveled internationally before, she decided to make light of the whole thing.

I gasped, held out my hand, palm forward in a halting stance. "No, Rhoda! No! Don't say that!"

It was too late; they had heard her and surrounded her. They led her back to the curtain.

Open-mouthed, I looked at the rest of the tour group whose jaws were dropped in astonishment like mine. I told them to proceed to the concourse. I would wait for Rhoda, and we would join them in a few minutes.

Ten minutes later she came out, red-faced, her hair mussed and a shirttail out on one side. I started to lecture her, but she held up her hand indignantly and said, "Don't say it! I promise that won't happen again." She whistled. "Whew! They bawled me out in there!" We continued to the boarding gate. I give her credit. In spite of her age, she made the trip easily.

The flight from Norfolk to Newark was about an hour and a half. The flight from Newark to Tel Aviv was a little over ten hours. It was an evening flight so that after the flight attendant served dinner we could try to sleep much of the way.

Israel is seven hours ahead of the US, so we arrived at nearly 5:00 p.m. Israeli time. Our guide and bus driver met us on the other side of Israeli customs and drove us to our hotel in Netanya. I don't sleep well on airplanes, so I went to bed early and slept soundly until 6:00 a.m.

Israel is not much larger than the state of New Jersey, so the longest drive we had between sites was about forty-five minutes. Most of the distances between sites were much shorter. It is easy to understand that travelers in Bible times walked from the mountains to the desert to the coast because they are in close proximity to each other.

Deuteronomy 11:11 (NKJV) describes Israel as a land of "hills and valleys." We went *up* to Jerusalem and *down* to the Dead Sea. Temperature variations were amazing. On one day it was forty-eight degrees in Jerusalem and nearly ninety degrees that afternoon at the Dead Sea.

It is impressive to stand on Mount Carmel where Elijah defeated the prophets of Baal and look out over the valley of Megiddo, perhaps the greatest battlefield in history. Its Greek pronunciation is a familiar term to most Christians: *Armageddon.*

Beit Shean knocked our socks off! It is the largest archaeological dig in Israel. The ruins stretch out far and wide, displaying a once commercial metropolis that was destroyed by an earthquake. Paved sidewalks and streets with drainage were at one time lined with merchandising shops. With artisan stonework and mosaic tiles still in place, we realized it must have been a beautiful city in its day.

We saw the archaeological site of Hazor. King Jabin led a confederation of Canaanite armies against Joshua. The accounts of the Judge Deborah commissioning Barak to lead an army and of Jael who heroically killed Jabin's general, Sisera, are told in this setting. It is fascinating to see the places where Old Testament biblical events took place.

However, it was the New Testament historical sites we focused on. These sites strengthened our faith and commitment, as demonstrated in the story of one of the men in our group.

ETHAN'S QUEST

Ethan and his wife Beth had joined our church four years earlier and made friends quickly. Their connections came about through our children's ministry, as they brought with them a lively seven-year-old son named Jessie. Love and concern for their children was the focus of a large group of young parents.

Ethan was a tall young man in his late thirties who had grown up in a church setting and was familiar with a regular worship attendance but now was beginning to struggle in his faith. There were so many things about the Bible, history, science, and Christianity he couldn't reconcile in his own mind. By this time, he had started a quest to make up his own mind about where he stood on so many things he had been taught growing up. He was not the type to give halfhearted devotion to anything, and he could no longer accept things simply because his parents did, nor could he teach Jessie precepts that he did not embrace himself.

I was amazed when I found out how much Ethan had read in the past few years. He was like a black hole sucking in information and assimilating it on the other side. From National Geographic to world politics to world history, Ethan immersed himself in as much knowledge as he could and seemed to retain it all. Even more impressive was that Ethan had read all four volumes of *The Works Of Flavious Josephus*, a record of Jewish history from 64 AD to 94 AD. Many preachers hesitate to take that project on.

He also loved to travel. He had visited Russia, India, Thailand, and Portugal. Now, he read the announcement that Kempsville Christian Church was hosting a Holy Land trip through Jerusalem Tours, Inc. He learned the church had hosted three successful tours previously through the same company and had confidence in the quality of the trip. The cost of the trip was a great value because it included airfare, meals, tickets to sites, an Israelite guide, and more. This trip provided another opportunity for travel and learning. So he registered himself and Beth, scheduled his parents to come stay with their son, and began to make preparations for the trip. All the while he hoped this trip would help him reconcile his faith with the struggle going on in his mind.

What were the doubts Ethan was wrestling with? There were several. *Why is there so much bloodshed and violence in Bible history? After having been copied repeatedly through centuries, how do we know our Bible today has integrity? Can I actually trust its counsel and commandments?* And the most important: *Was Jesus actually the Son of God, or was He simply an ordinary man elevated to divine status, the way others were in pagan religions?*

On this trip, Ethan would discover what it meant to be a disciple of Jesus. He would walk where Jesus walked, see what Jesus saw, and hear the teachings of Christ through Scripture readings. He would sail across the Sea of Galilee as the disciples did with Jesus more than two centuries earlier.

THE TEAM

Our team consisted of eighteen people: two preachers with their wives and fourteen church members, most of whom were long-time Christians. Sandi and I were not the only ones to have made the tour previously; Terry and Kathy Barton made a second trip with us and had convinced their neighbors, Jerry and Roxanne, to join us. There was a variety of ages in the group. Ethan and Beth were the youngest.

With a master's degree in geology, our guide was a valuable resource of information. Kobi (Jacobi) had grown up in Israel and met his American wife on a tour, and the two of them shared a home in Florida six months while he led tours throughout Israel the other six months. He, along with our bus driver, Avi (Abrahim), took us throughout the small yet unfathomable country of Israel. Ethan peppered Kobi with questions about the political and economic conditions of the country. He wanted to know how the borders of Israel were maintained, how the currency related to the international market, which political party seemed to be the strongest. An educated and experienced tour guide, Kobi was up to the task and patiently satisfied Ethan's hunger for information.

One day we visited Israel's largest archaeological site, Beit Shean, one of the most ancient of Israel's cities. As Ethan looked out over the ruins of this ancient city he could imagine a bustling metropolis. Some pillars still stood, while others lay where they had fallen. A theatre and bathhouse with running water were still nearly intact. Ethan could imagine people walking up and down the main street, the "cardo," visiting shops along the sides of the road. He was impressed the road was constructed with a built-in drainage system. He was amazed the home builders had inserted open transoms over the doors for light and ventilation and in the walls what seemed to be dampers to allow some flexibility for earth tremors. The Roman baths that dispersed heat throughout the room demonstrated an understanding of heat conduction. For years Ethan had thought these ancient peoples were primitive with low intelligence but now realized they were actually brilliant. Our discoveries in modern construction have been built on the backs of their discoveries. He remembered Sir Isaac Newton had written, "If I have seen further it is by standing on ye shoulders of Giants."

Kobi caught Ethan's attention as he spoke to the group, reading 1 Samuel 31 and pointing out that it was here the Philistines found the dead body of king Saul, beheaded it, and exposed it on the walls of Beit Shean (Beth Shan). Ethan recalled in his mind the battles, wars, and bloodshed he had read of in the Old Testament that were distasteful to him. Kobi went on to say, "David courageously led his forces to reclaim the body of Israel's king and treated it with respect. This put David in high honor among the people." Then he reminded us, "The Bible says David was a man after God's own heart [Acts 13:22]."

Ethan turned to me. "Why was there so much bloodshed in the Bible, and how could the warrior king David be a man after God's own heart? Was the God of the Bible a warrior god? Wasn't David an adulterer? How can we say David was a man after God's own heart?"

"No, the God of the Bible is not a warrior god," I said. After a bit of a pause, "You have to remember we're talking about a period of time before Christ. They hadn't heard the Beatitudes, the Sermon on the Mount. Jesus made the difference, but He hadn't come yet. It was early in the nation's history, and they were surrounded by heathens who *were* warlike. The Israelites were people who had been commanded by God to reclaim a land He had given to Abraham, their ancestor. This was important, because it was in this place and through these people God would bring the Messiah, the Savior."

"But why so much bloodshed?" Ethan asked.

I tried to give a brief but accurate answer. "In order to bring the Messiah through Israel, they had to be a people of one God. The nations who occupied the land after Abraham were pagans who worshiped many gods. Their heathen worship was horrible with prostitution, incest, and even child sacrifice. They had to be driven out of the land so all Israel would be a people of one God: Jehovah God. Of course, the pagans rejected Israel's God and attacked."

"And David, a man after God's own heart?"

"So, David *was*, in fact, a warrior. But he was a man after God's heart, not because he was so pure, so good a man, but because he wanted to honor God. Other rulers were only interested in their own honor, not God's."

Ethan understood and nodded. "And David even raised the funds to build the temple . . . *because* he wanted to honor God."

"Right. And *God did not allow* David to build the temple *because* his hands had shed so much blood" (1 Chronicles 22:8).

Later we stopped at Banias, an ancient site at the base of Mount Hermon. Mount Hermon's snowcapped peak provided much of the water that flowed into the Jordan. At the foot of the mountain, a beautiful spring trickled by a one-time pagan temple to the Greek god Pan, then flowed into the Banias river, which emptied into the Jordan river. Into the solid face of the rock a niche had been carved to hold a shrine of Pan. On a recent trip to Greece, Sandi and I had seen the kinds of images and icons dedicated to Pan, most of them immoral by our standards.

Kobi called on one of the tourists to read Matthew 16:13–18 from his Bible. He read aloud:

When Jesus came to the region of Caesarea Philippi, he asked his disciples, "Who do people say the Son of Man is?"

They replied, "Some say John the Baptist; others say Elijah; and still others, Jeremiah or one of the prophets."

"But what about you?" he asked. "Who do you say I am?"

Simon Peter answered, "You are the Messiah, the Son of the living God."

Jesus replied, "Blessed are you, Simon son of Jonah, for this was not revealed to you by flesh and blood, but by my Father in heaven. And I tell you that you are Peter, and on this rock I will build my church, and the gates of Hades will not overcome it."

As Kobi read that passage, Ethan thought, *Imagine, right here, in front of a pagan temple in which a pagan god was worshipped in immorality, Jesus challenged his disciples, "Who do you say I am?" The disciples were on the spot; they had to declare themselves as believers or following Jesus made no sense. A profession of faith in Jesus here would require courage and conviction. Peter boldly stepped forward, "You are the Messiah, the Son of the living God." Jesus approved Peter's confession.*

While the rest of the team wandered about the site, Ethan examined the niche where the statue of the pagan god had stood and thought how intimidating it must have been to make that public profession of faith before friends and neighbors who worshiped those gods. Suddenly, this tour became intensely personal. He knew he lived in a time and place where multiculturalism was prominent. He lived next to people who were of either other faiths or no particular faith at all. He worked in a large corporation beside Hindis, Buddhists, Muslims, Protestants, and Catholics. He wondered, *Have I ever spoken of my Christian faith to them? . . . No, I didn't want to offend them.*

> *But thanks be to God, who always leads us as captives in Christ's triumphal procession and uses us to spread the aroma of the knowledge of him everywhere. For we are to God the pleasing aroma of Christ among those who are being saved and those who are perishing. To the one we are an aroma that brings death; to the other, an aroma that brings life. And who is equal to such a task? Unlike so many, we do not peddle the word of God for profit. On the contrary, in Christ we speak before God with sincerity, as those sent from God.*
>
> 2 Corinthians 2:14–17

Ethan knew he would never be at peace until he settled this issue. He rejoined the team, and we returned to the hotel.

The next day our driver took us to a number of sites and then to Yardenit, a baptismal site located in the Jordan River in northern Israel. On our way I recalled a humorous event from a previous trip. A group of nearly fifty people from an Africa tour stood on the platform waiting to follow us, their minister growing impatient. I took the professions of faith from the two in my group who wanted to be baptized and gently lowered them into the water and raised them up again. As we walked up the ramp to exit the river, a black man from Africa approached me and said, "I want you to baptize me."

I was pleasantly surprised. "You want *me* to baptize you?"

"Yes," he said.

Thrilled with this opportunity, I led him down the ramp, took his profession of faith, lowered him into the water, and raised him up out of it. The man rubbed his eyes, looked up toward heaven with his arms lifted, said something in Portuguese, and then dropped his arms around my shoulders, embracing me. We exchanged addresses and promised to keep in touch.

I looked over to the African group thinking the preacher would be rejoicing as well. He wasn't. If anything he looked annoyed. He led his group down the ramp and baptized them one by one. It was then I realized *why* this man wanted me to baptize him.

The African preacher reached out, grabbed the first candidate, a woman, pulled her over in front of himself, spun her around, placed his hands on her shoulders, and jumped up aggressively, pushing her down into the water. As she went under, her arms went flailing upward desperately, splashing water everywhere. Then the preacher pulled her up by the shoulders of her baptismal gown and shoved her away while grabbing the next person in line.

So, THAT'S why he wanted me to baptize him. Still a favorite memory, it will always remind me that who we're baptized by is not as important as the One we're baptized into (1 Corinthians 1:11–13).

Yardenit is a picturesque swelling of the Jordan River used as a baptismal site. Today, the Jordan River is barely more than a stream, but at Yardenit a dam was built to widen and deepen the baptismal area. Surrounded by trees and accompanied by trained doves, it provides a beautiful setting to confirm one's commitment to Christ.

Several in our group had declared they wanted to be baptized in the Jordan. However, by the time we arrived, eleven people from our group of eighteen had made the decision, among them Ethan's wife, Beth. Ethan stood on the upper platform as he watched them walk down the ramp that led into the cold water and shiver. As the baptism took place, Ethan noticed something move in the water, then he heard Terry call out, "Look, there's a fish!" Ethan looked where Terry was pointing and saw a fish over two feet long swim behind me.

"It's a catfish!" Terry exclaimed.

Ethan smiled. "That's just great, isn't it? John the Baptist gets doves; Randy gets a catfish!"

Terry guffawed.

Beth's movement caught his attention as she moved forward to me. I asked her to profess her faith in Jesus, splashed some water on the robe between her shoulder blades to get her acclimated to the cold, then raised my hand upward. "Beth, because of your profession of faith in Jesus, I baptize you into Christ in the name of the Father, the Son, and the Holy Ghost." I placed one hand behind her back and gently lowered her backward into the water and lifted her up again. Beth threw her arms around my neck, hugged me, and started making her way up the ramp out of the water, hugging each person in line behind her.

Ethan walked to the ramp to meet her with a towel. As he watched her come near, he knew she wanted him to be a devoted to follower of Christ as she was. He knew she wanted her family to be Christian, her children to be raised in the Lord, but he couldn't commit to Christ for her sake. He had to make the decision for himself.

Less than half an hour from Yardenit we boarded a boat to sail across the Sea of Galilee. It was a beautiful day, cool with a light breeze. Praise songs were played over the boat's public address system, and then I spoke to the group.

"Here we are on the Sea of Galilee, a place we've read about in our Bibles almost all our lives." I raised my arm, pointed my finger to the shore, and in a sweeping motion pointed all around the perimeter of the sea. "As we come here we realize so much of Jesus' ministry was focused on the villages around the water. The Bible says great crowds of people were following Jesus, and He became concerned for his disciples. He sent them to the other side of the sea while He went up on the mountain to pray." I pointed to a mountain off in the distance.

"But a storm came upon them, the wind, which was channeled through the mountains, stirred the sea and threatened to overturn the boat. These experienced fishermen were frightened for their lives. They had lost sight of Jesus and assumed they were powerless against the storm. That's the way it is when we go through trouble; we develop tunnel vision, seeing only the problem and not the solution.

"In the midst of the storm, the disciples saw Jesus walking on the water toward them. He had never taken His eyes from them. The disciples were frightened of Him at first. But Jesus said, 'It is I. Don't be afraid.' Peter responded, 'Lord, if it is You, let me come to You on the water.' And Jesus said, 'Come.' Peter stepped out of the boat and at first walked on water, but taking his eyes off Jesus and focusing on the wind and waves, he started to sink. Peter prayed the shortest prayer: 'Lord, save me!' I can think of a shorter prayer: 'HELP!' Jesus reached out to Peter and pulled him to safety. The disciples couldn't see Jesus in the storm, but He could see them from the mountaintop and came to them. Peter took his eyes off Jesus, but Jesus never took his eyes off Peter." Then I told them how this event reminds us to stay focused on the Lord.

One of our travelers, Mike, led us in a few praise songs followed by a time of quiet meditation. On each tour, it seems as if the boat ride across the Sea of Galilee has a profound spiritual impact on everyone. That impact was felt by Ethan as well. Ethan worked his way to the bow of the boat, away from the others. Beth joined him, sitting in front of him and leaning into his arms. They didn't talk. In fact, no one talked. This was a time of meditation.

For Ethan, this experience on the Sea of Galilee gave a sense of "realism" to the Gospels. These were real places and involved real people. He could imagine Jesus visiting one fishing village after another, teaching the Word of God, performing miracles and drawing disciples to himself. Everything felt so . . . *real*. Ethan was silent for the next hour or so.

One of the most exciting sites we visited was Qumran. It was here the famous Dead Sea Scrolls were found. Qumran was a Jewish settlement of Essenes, who had isolated themselves from popular city life to live in communes similar to a monastery. Nearly 200 people practiced their isolationist faith there, studying the Scriptures which were written on scrolls and observing their rituals.

In 1947, a Bedouin shepherd boy discovered a series of scrolls that have been reported to be the greatest archaeological discovery to date. Dr. Bryant Wood writes,

> Probably the Dead Sea Scrolls have had the greatest Biblical impact. They have provided Old Testament manuscripts approximately 1,000 years older than our previous oldest manuscript. The Dead Sea Scrolls have demonstrated that the Old Testament was accurately transmitted during this interval. In addition, they provide a wealth of information on the times leading up to, and during, the life of Christ.[6]

Since the original finds were in Jerusalem, Ethan studied the sample copies of the scrolls in the Qumran museum, read the signage with each

---

[6] Will Varner, PhD, "What is the importance of the Dead Sea Scrolls?" *Associates for Bible Research*, May, 21, 2008, http://www.biblearchaeology.org/post/2008/05/What-is-the-importance-of-the-Dead-Sea-Scrolls.aspx#Article.

display, and realized that with the exception of a few minor details, the Bible we possess today has integrity and is a reliable copy. While he couldn't read the original Hebrew, he knew he was looking at actual evidence of the Bible's trustworthiness. His confidence in the authenticity of the Bible was reinforced. By great leaps, it seemed his faith was being substantiated.

That afternoon we made our trip to Jerusalem, stopping at an overlook for a panoramic view of the city three miles away. The white walls separated the old city from the modern city which surrounded it. From our perspective we could see an olive tree grove, the Mount of Olives, and the Kidron Valley that ran along the eastern wall. However, the most obvious point of interest was the golden Dome of the Rock, which sat on the Temple Mount. All of Jerusalem was a gorgeous sight to behold, and even today the parcel of land it occupies may be the most important piece of land in the entire world. Joel Rosenberg calls it "the Epicenter."[72] America, Russia, China—nearly every major power on earth is focused on this forty-eight-square-mile parcel of Jerusalem. Compared to New York City's 300 square miles, Jerusalem seems small. However, its influence is greater than that of any other city in the world.

Ethan had already resolved many of his concerns. He now accepted the validity of the Bible, but he wondered about his thoughts of Jesus: *Was Jesus a mere man, or was He more? Was He, in fact, the Son of God?* Ethan didn't consider his thoughts to be irreligious; there was no superior attitude with them. He didn't want to offend God, but he had questions. *How can we know?* He was like the father who pleaded with Jesus, "Lord, I believe; help me overcome my unbelief" (Mark 9:24).

Even John the Baptist had questions. While in prison awaiting his death, John sent a couple of his disciples to ask Jesus, "Are you the one?" (Matthew 11:2–6). Ethan was simply asking the same question: *Jesus, are you the one?* He had to know if the claims of *Jesus* were true and if they warranted his devotion.

---

[7] Joel C. Rosenberg, *Epicenter: Why the Current Rumblings in the Middle East Will Change Your Future*, Oasis Audio, 2008.

MOUNT OF OLIVES

We started our day at the Mount of Olives, took a group photo before the overlook, and began walking down the steep road toward Jerusalem. When Jesus approached Jerusalem from the Mount of Olives in Matthew 11, crowds of people thronged around Him shouting praise to God:

"Blessed is the king who comes in the name of the Lord!"

"Peace in heaven and glory in the highest!"

Some of the Pharisees in the crowd said to Jesus, "Teacher, rebuke your disciples!"

"I tell you," he replied, "if they keep quiet, the stones will cry out." (Luke 19:38–41)

The stones will cry out . . . The stones have a testimony, Ethan thought. *I wonder what they will say.*

THE GARDEN OF GETHSEMANE

The end of our path from the mount took us to an olive tree grove marked the Garden of Gethsemane. In his mind's eye, Ethan could imagine Jesus prostrate beneath the twisted trees, praying He would not have to drink the cup of suffering before Him. The gnarled appearance of the trees seemed appropriate for the upheaval of emotions Jesus must have experienced. It was here Jesus was arrested and taken to Annas and then to Caiaphas for trial.

Crowds of people walked the path that encircled the grove and led to the Church of All Nations, a beautiful cathedral marking the site where Jesus prayed. While we don't agree with much of Catholic teaching, we still owe a great deal of gratitude to the Catholic Church because they have preserved so many biblical sites, usually by placing a church on them.

As we walked the path in sync with the crowd, Ethan was impressed with the humble reverence of so many people. Usually crowds are noisy, boisterous. There's almost always a couple of unruly people. But not here. They were solemn and reverent as they considered the place where Jesus had suffered and prayed.

We entered the old city through the Dung Gate, so named because it was probably used to convey garbage to the valley of Hinnom to be incinerated. The old city of Jerusalem is divided into four main quarters. Ethan stood nearly in the middle of the five-acre plaza looking at the Western (Wailing) Wall to his right, the Jewish quarter to his left, the Christian and Armenian quarters to his far left, and the Muslim quarter ahead of him. He knew he was standing in the middle of a plaza that formed the foundation of three major world religions: Judaism, Christianity, and Islam. As important as this was, he also knew that, for him, this trip was about *his* faith in Jesus.

On the walls of the city he could see a line of demarcation separating what was said to be original stone from reconstruction stone. Yet each stone, regardless of its placement, seemed to speak the name of Jesus. As Jesus said, "The stones cried out." You could not separate the history of this city from the name of Jesus.

We followed a path from Gethsemane to the House of Caiaphas, the high priest intent on Jesus' death. Kobi reminded us that Jesus was taken to the house of Caiaphas in order to find a reason worthy of execution. Ethan already knew they couldn't find such a reason and actually employed witnesses to testify against Jesus. The chief priests and the whole Sanhedrin were looking for false evidence against Jesus so that they could put Him to death. But they did not find any, though many false witnesses came forward (Matthew 26:59–60).

We walked down a stone cut stairway into a dungeon beneath the house where Jesus would have been held, awaiting trial. The small room was a crude, carved-out section of rock wall that seemed to close in on us. It was dark and depressing. We read Scripture, we sang, and holding hands, we prayed. Jesus was led from Caiaphas to the Sanhedrin and eventually to Pilate, who pronounced the death sentence on Jesus.

There are two sites generally recognized as possible places where Jesus was crucified, buried, and resurrected: the Garden Tomb and the Church of the Holy Sepulchre. We visited both.

The Garden Tomb was "outside the city" (Hebrews 13:12) and looks the way I would imagine it looked in Jesus' day. We saw a craggy rock formation from the quarry that had been a source of stones used for the construction of the temple. As we looked at that rocky mount, we could see what had been interpreted as eyes and a mouth, giving it the nickname "the place of the skull" (Matthew 27:33).

Just a few hundred yards away was a beautiful setting that featured a rock-hewn tomb some believe to be the burial place of Jesus. A trough to accommodate a large circular stone had been cut at the entrance. It was easy to imagine a stone rolling into place and then being sealed with Rome's official stamp.

A great number of people who had come in groups lined up to enter the tomb and see the place where the body of Jesus may have lain. Ethan walked in with Beth. They stood for a few moments and looked at two unoccupied stone slabs. Someone had placed a sign on the wall between them: *He is not here. He is risen.*

As he exited the tomb, Ethan wondered, *Where is the body of Jesus?* He remembered the previous Easter's sermon: *If the disciples had stolen the body and knew the resurrection was fake, they would not have died giving their lives for something they knew to be a lie. If the enemies had the body, they would have produced it to stop the growth of Christianity. They would have said, "See? He is dead." Where is the body?* Ethan looked back toward Golgotha. *They couldn't have gone to the wrong tomb. So where is the body? Why is it in 2,000 years, with so many discoveries, they have found nothing to indicate Jesus is dead?*

After visiting the tomb, we were led to a private chamber in which we could meditate and observe communion. I gave a brief devotion. "On an earlier tour, I had a chance to talk with the garden guide, who drew my attention to an iron deposit on the upper left hand side of the tomb's entrance. 'What is that?' I asked.

"'That, brother, was an exciting discovery.' He walked to the tomb and put his finger on the place. 'At first, we thought it was shrapnel from one of the wars that took place here. But last summer, a team of researchers from the University of Tennessee took a sample and dated it back to the first century.' Pointing to the blot on the stone tomb, he looked at me and smiled. 'This is the remains of an iron spike that secured the round stone in place and prevented it from rolling open.'

"All of a sudden I realized what this meant. It meant when the angel rolled away the stone, the spike that secured the stone in place was sheared off! That's the power in His resurrection! . . . He's alive!"

He's alive! Ethan thought. *After all these years, no one has been able to produce the body or find evidence that Jesus is dead. Of course He's alive!*

We walked the Via Dolorosa (the Way of Sorrow), believed to be the road Jesus walked to Golgotha, stopping along the way to note nine "stations of the cross." Small plaques on the walls marked places where Jesus fell for the first time, gave his cross to Simon of Cyrene, where he fell for the second and third times, etc.

Hustle and bustle from the shops lining the road echoed against the stone walls. Merchants called out to us trying to draw us into their small shops to buy their wares. The noise made us think what it must have been like for Christ to walk that path in the midst of sorrow and weeping from friends and taunting from unbelievers.

Our next visit was the Church of the Holy Sepulchre, the site where most authorities believe Jesus actually died and was buried. We were surprised to see hundreds of people in the courtyard, some waiting to enter the church, others standing in circles holding hands and praying, and still others standing in groups sharing their thoughts with one another.

Inside, even more people, perhaps thousands, walked the halls of the ancient cathedral that dated back to the fourth, perhaps the third century. The grand architecture, artwork, icons all contributed to a spiritual atmosphere. The numbers of people who walked the vestibules were ardent believers in Christ. The testimony of this structure and the people within it was almost overpowering. Again, Ethan wondered, *So many people. People from every nation. People of all ages from all walks of life. How could one ordinary man with twelve disciples affect so many? But Jesus was not ordinary.*

Ethan walked through the crowds holding Beth's hand so they wouldn't get separated, but his eyes were darting from place to place. He looked up at the grand arches of the cathedral ceiling that seemed to direct his attention upward to God. He looked at the artwork that lined the walls, listened to the buzz of so many people praying, all of which seemed to be a familiar profession—the profession he had made when he was baptized as a ten-year-old child: "I believe Jesus is the Christ, the Son of the living God." His mind was filled with so much information, so many sites and testimonies. His heart was burning. He felt a powerful desire to connect with God in a way he had never connected before. He pulled Beth close and wrapped his arms around her and whispered in her ear, "I can't wait to tell Jessie about this trip and why she needs to know Jesus. Jesus is so alive to me right now."

Afterword

I hope this book has demonstrated how exciting and fulfilling ministry for Christ can be. I didn't realize this until I came out of ministry for nearly six years. My father had become ill and required multiple surgeries. He needed help operating three shoe stores that employed twenty people. Unbeknown to him, for a few months I had been going through a time of soul-searching, wondering if I was really called for ministry. When Dad asked me if I wanted to move back to my hometown and help until he recovered, I saw this as an opportunity to get clarity in my life. Was I, in fact, cut out for ministry or perhaps for something else?

During my time in the secular marketplace, I continued serving the Lord, but on a smaller scale. I helped plant and build a new church, served as an elder, and taught Sunday school. Yet, my new career never felt right *for me*. We lived well in a nice home and neighborhood, but I wasn't satisfied. I wanted the church to grow and thrive. While I had a small part in that, it wasn't enough. As I drove from one store to another, managing inventory and employees, I would think of a good sermon topic but never get the opportunity to preach it. It was similar to the adage, "I have money burning a hole in my pocket. I've got to spend it!" Maybe an even better saying is, "I've got an itch that I can't scratch." I never felt I was doing enough to help the church, and there was a growing restlessness to my spirit.

My dissatisfaction must have been obvious to my family, because they often talked about full-time church work. Finally, one day, out of the clear blue with no prompting, our eleven-year-old son, Todd, approached me and said, "Dad, I think it's time . . . you should get back in the ministry." One thing I always appreciated about our sons was that they always enjoyed attending and participating in church. We never had to *force* them to attend.

For me, that was all it took. My father was doing well and was ready to assume control of the shoe stores again. Sandi and I discussed it and made the decision to re-enter full-time ministry.

At the time, I was one of the directors of the Virginia Evangelizing Fellowship, an organization that would go into an area of Virginia and lay the foundation and build the frame and roof of a new church building. Hundreds of workers from across the state would give one to two weeks working day and night until a building was under roof. Then the local congregation would finish it. At one of the monthly directors' meetings, I asked if anyone knew of an open church in Virginia that could support a family of five. Two available churches were mentioned, one only two hours away from my parents and another all the way across the state in Virginia Beach, over eight hours away.

I sent my resume to both churches, hoping to hear from the one closest to my hometown. I heard right away from Kempsville Christian Church in Virginia Beach but heard nothing from the other. After several phone conversations, the elders at Kempsville invited me to preach and go through the interview process. I accepted the invitation, and Sandi and I drove to Virginia Beach on a Thanksgiving weekend while our sons stayed with my parents.

We met the wonderful people of this church and fell in love with them. More than that, the chairman of the elders walked me out to an empty lot adjacent to the church building and said, "We hope one day the church will grow to the point that we fill all this land with facilities to serve the Lord." That challenged me and excited me at the same time. God had led me to a church that actually wanted to grow! Many churches are content with maintaining the status quo, keeping things the way they are with their network of personal connections. Here was a church that wanted to reach their community with the gospel!

The interview seemed to go well, and Kempsville invited me to accept the ministry beginning in January. Still waiting for a response from the other church, I asked for a week of prayer. However, no response from the church closer to my hometown came. One month after sending my resume, I accepted the position in Virginia Beach and started making plans to transition across the state. *Then* my letter to the other church came back to me—unopened. It had never been delivered! No one was there to receive it and respond to it. I took that as leading from God that He wanted me at Kempsville, and for thirty years I never questioned whether I was where God wanted me.

What a blessing those years at Kempsville have been to me. They were not always easy years; there were many challenges. But I always had the support of the leadership and the fulfillment of ministry. At one point, while searching for a youth minister, they approached me about hiring Josh, our second son, and we did. By the time I announced my retirement, Josh had served on staff with me for fifteen years, and the leadership then approached him and asked him to assume the senior ministry, giving him the encouragement and support they had given me.

Now, more than thirty years later, I see the church continuing to focus on the Lord and continuing to grow. People are coming to Christ. Ministry groups are multiplying. Outreach is extending further into the region. This blesses my heart immensely.

Ministry is unlike anything else you could choose for a vocation. In the secular world, you work with employers and employees, but in ministry, you work with volunteers who give of their time and resources to partner with you. Volunteers can come and go of their own free will because they don't depend on a paycheck. Ministry, however, requires patience, perseverance, integrity, communication skills, courage, and creativity. And it never gets boring!

Ministry is not easy, *but it is fulfilling.* I have conducted weddings of couples who were the children of marriages I had conducted years earlier. I've watched children mature and take their place alongside their parents serving the Lord. And on the other side of the coin the church staff and I have faced difficult challenges in paying off our worship center, children's center, and fellowship hall. We've faced challenges in helping people work out their conflicts in friendships and marriages. We've faced challenges in maintaining ministries when the economy of the area was poor. However, it was in those challenges we grew in faith and in ministry and found joy in fulfillment.

There's nothing more exciting and fulfilling than seeing God work. **Remarkable things still happen in the kingdom of God!** People who have no hope of a future are given new life in Christ. I've seen drug addicts, prostitutes, and convicted felons become dedicated people of faith. I've seen the Word of God convict and draw people to Christ.

After one sermon, I went to the church foyer to greet people and a teenage boy confronted me: "Have you been talking to my mother?!"

I smiled. "No, but I think your mother has been talking to the Lord and the Lord is talking to you."

I've seen three generations of families serve the Lord. I've seen a small church pay off a million-dollar building in five years. Through the Lord's blessings and the generosity of the membership, I've seen Kempsville fund the building of two churches in communist China. (One had been destroyed by a flood and the other by a snowstorm.) Remarkable things *do* still happen.

And fellowship—I could never have survived thirty years at one church without the support and friendship of so many men and women who loved the Lord. Any success at Kempsville was due to a wonderful fellowship of men and women, boys and girls who loved the Lord and had a mind to serve (Nehemiah 4:6).

In closing this book, I want to encourage people to enter ministry. If not vocational ministry, I urge you to get involved in your local church, to enter a fellowship of believers who love the Lord and want to do exciting things for Him. Serve in whatever capacity God makes available to you.

You may become disheartened from time to time, but when you look back on your life, you won't regret making yourself available to Christ. As I pray for the ministry of this book, I'm praying for you.

God bless you.

Randy Childress

Printed in the United States
By Bookmasters